A Writer's Guide

to

Sassy Synonyms

for "Said"

Second Edition

Other books by Creative Works Publishing

Captive Love
Stormy Desires
The Hope Chest
Pursuit of Passion
ABCs to Positive Living
Quit Smoking using the Time Chart System
No Need to Fear: Overcoming Panic Disorder

A Writer's Guide

to

Sassy Synonyms

for "Said"

Second Edition

Koz St. Christopher
Victoria St. Christopher

Creative Works Publishing
Canton, Ohio

Printed in the United States of America on acid-free paper
Cover design by Koz St. Christopher

Library of Congress Cataloging-in-Publication Data

St. Christopher, Koz, 1958–
  A writer's guide to sassy synonyms for "said" / Koz and Victoria
M.
  St. Christopher.
    p. cm.
  ISBN 1-930693-89-3 (pbk. : alk. paper)
  1. English language--Synonyms and antonyms. 2. Say (The
English
  word)
  I. St. Christopher, Victoria M., 1953–
  II. Title.
PE1599.S29 S8 2001
423'.1--dc21

                                            2001000031

About This Book

This guide, which functions not only as a dictionary and thesaurus, also gives useful examples on how to use each word in a practical manner. It was created to assist writers who wish to expand their choice of descriptive words, offering over 1,000 substitutes for the word *said* when writing fiction, nonfiction, poetry, etc.

This handy reference book comes complete with a *Quick Reference Guide* which lists all the boldface words and was developed in such a fashion so as to assist writers not only in finding descriptive, colorful alternatives for the word *said*, but also to offer other options similar in meaning. Each boldface word is followed by one or more definitions, additional synonyms and a sample sentence meant to demonstrate its usage.

It is the authors' fervent hope that *A Writer's Guide to Sassy Synonyms for "Said"* will be an invaluable tool in the creation of every writer's literary masterpieces.

-A a-

Abjured: renounced under oath; recanted solemnly. Abandoned; disallowed; disavowed; disclaimed; deserted; gave up; recanted; rejected; renounced; repudiated. *"I know that I told the police I did it, but I didn't kill him,"* abjured Erica tearfully, *"I didn't kill him!"*

Acceded: consent granted, often at the insistence of another. Agreed to; approved; conceded; concurred with; granted; permitted. *"Very well,"* mother acceded, *"you may stay out past your curfew just this once."*

Accepted: regarded as proper, right, true or usual. Answered affirmatively. Agreed to. Endured resignedly or patiently. Confirmed; customary; established; standard; time-honored; went along with. *"All right, she didn't do it,"* accepted the detective reluctantly. *"But if she's innocent the question remains, who did kill the old man?"*

Acclaimed: praised enthusiastically and often times publicly. Applauded; approved of loudly; cheered; commended; extolled; hailed; lauded. *"Here's to two people who deserve all the love and happiness life has to offer,"* acclaimed the best man raising his glass.*

Accused: charged with a shortcoming or error; charged with wrongdoing against another. Arraigned; blamed; charged; cited; indicted. *"It was Jonathan!"* accused Keri. *"He's the one responsible for that poor old man's untimely death."*

Acknowledged: admitted or declared the existence, reality or truth of. Expressed gratitude, recognition or thanks for. Made a statement reluctantly, often times regarding something previously denied or doubted. Accepted; admitted; confessed; owned up to. *"Were it not for the tireless effort of Mr. Jones,"* acknowledged the chairman of the board, *"this project would never have come to fruition."*

Acquiesced: complied or consented passively or without protest.

Reconciled or resigned oneself to. Agreed; bowed to; capitulated; complied; gave in; submitted; yielded. *"I'll do whatever you want,"* *acquiesced the terrified bank teller, "just please don't kill me."*

Added: said further; made or created an addition. Attached; appended; offered in addition; summed up; supplemented; tacked on at the end. *"Besides," Derek added, his cold eyes hungry with greed, "no one will ever know, unless one of us rats the others out."*

Addressed: made or gave a formal speech to. Directed a spoken comment to another's attention. Greeted; lectured; orated; saluted in words; spoke to; talked to. *"Ladies and gentlemen of the jury, you will disregard the defendant's outrageous behavior during this trial," addressed the judge sternly.*

Adhered: remained constant, faithful, loyal or true. Clung to; held closely to; maintained; stood by; stuck fast to. *"Despite all the evidence to the contrary, I still believe in my client's innocence," adhered the attorney stubbornly.*

Adjured: appealed to or entreated earnestly. Commanded or directed solemnly, as under oath. *"Please," adjured the worried mother, "tell me where I can find my daughter."*

Admired: viewed or regarded with approval, pleasure or wonder; held in high esteem or regard; thought highly of. Esteemed; praised; prized; respected; valued. *"She's beautiful, intelligent and funny," admired Jake. "She's everything I've ever wanted in a woman."*

Admitted: granted to be real, true or valid. Acknowledged; conceded, confessed; declared; professed. *"I did it," admitted the old man resignedly, "I shot him in cold blood."*

Admonished: reminded of a duty or obligation. Advised; cautioned; chided; chastened; criticized; rebuked; reprimanded; reproached; reproved gently. *"What you did was wrong," the old woman* *admonished, "and it is your responsibility to make amends."*

Advised: offered advice or an opinion. Admonished; apprised; counseled; encouraged; exhorted; informed; made known; notified; recommended; suggested; urged. *"I feel it is in your best interest to accept the plea bargain," advised the young attorney.*

Advocated: spoke out for, pleaded or argued in favor of, pleaded the cause of. Backed; campaigned for; endorsed; favored; promoted; supported; urged. *"In the face of certain heinous crimes, the death penalty is the only just solution," advocated the prosecuting attorney.*

Affirmed: declared firmly or positively, or formally and solemnly, but not under sworn oath. Upheld the validity of. Asserted; claimed; confirmed; contended; declared; maintained; professed. *"It is my opinion," Dr. James affirmed grimly, "that lack of exercise and proper diet are factors which compounded your health problems."*

Agreed: granted consent. Came to an understanding or the same conclusion. Went along with, saw eye to eye. Acceded; accorded; assented; chimed; concurred; harmonized; jibed. *"The slogan is perfect," agreed Amy. "I wouldn't change a thing."*

Alerted: notified of approaching action or danger. Informed; notified; made aware of; signaled; warned. *"It's the cops," alerted the lookout fearfully. "They're almost here!"*

Alleged: stated or expressed positively without or before proof. Stated in support or denial of a claim or accusation. Accused; affirmed; asserted; charged; claimed; contended; declared. *"The crime," alleged the reporter, "was committed by a young man known only as Timmy."*

Allowed: let happen, gave into. Gave permission. Admitted; approved; asserted; authorized; gave; granted; sanctioned. *"If a state university is really where you want to go," allowed mother, "then I'll abide by* *your wishes."*

Alluded: made an indirect reference to; touched upon. Hinted; intimated; mentioned; spoke of. *"Perhaps he's not as innocent as he would have you believe," alluded the detective.*

Amended: changed for the better by adding, deleting or rephrasing. Altered; bettered; changed; corrected; improved; modified; rectified; revised. *"What I meant to say," Sara amended, "is that while I find Max to be a talented artist, I don't feel he is right for this job."*

Announced: made something known formally or publicly. Proclaimed the presence of. Advertised; broadcast; declared; disclosed; foretold; revealed. *"I have some terrific news," announced John to all his friends. "Marie has agreed to be my wife."*

Answered: spoke, wrote or acted in response to. Replied; responded; retorted; solved. *"As I already told you," the defendant answered calmly, "I was with my girlfriend the night of the murders."*

Appealed: made an earnest or urgent entreaty or request. Begged; beseeched; entreated; pleaded; supplicated. *"The only just thing to do in this case," appealed the defense attorney, "is to acquit my client of all charges."*

Applauded: expressed approval of or commended highly. Acclaimed; complimented; congratulated; lauded; praised. *"You were wonderful," applauded Jane. "I've never seen a more convincing Juliet."*

Approved: spoke or thought favorably of. Considered good or worthy. Accepted; concurred; confirmed; endorsed; sanctioned. *"Your choice of colors is excellent," approved Chris. "I couldn't have done better myself."*

Argued: put forth reasons for or against. Asserted; contended; debated; disputed; held; maintained. *"But dad," Jason argued, "just* *because you went to college doesn't mean it's right for me."*

Articulated: expressed clearly, distinctly and coherently. Conveyed; enunciated; pronounced; stated; uttered; voiced. *"The truth you seek," articulated the shriveled old gnome, "can be found in the cave of Life and Death."*

Ascertained: learned about through examination, investigation or experimentation. Discovered; detected; established; unearthed; verified. *"Despite your alibi, the real mastermind behind the jewelry heist," ascertained the detective, "is you, Mr. Smith."*

Ascribed: attributed to a specific cause, origin or source. Credited; related; traced to. *"The root of all our problems is lack of backers for this project," ascribed the president of the company."*

Asked: put a question to or made a request of or for. Sought an answer to or information about. Begged; entreated; implored; inquired; quizzed; requested. *"Is it true," Bethany asked hesitantly, "is Kevin responsible for setting the fire that killed those people?"*

Aspired: had great ambition. Hoped, hungered, longed or yearned for. Craved; desired; pursued; sought. *"One of these days," aspired the young musician, "people all over the world will know my name."*

Assailed: attacked verbally; set upon violently. Assaulted; attacked. *"You killed her, you monster!" assailed the distraught young woman. "You killed my baby!"*

Assented: agreed with another's actions, opinions or views especially after some deliberation or discussion. Acceded; accorded; conceded; concurred; consented; corroborated. *"After carefully reviewing Bob's recommendations, we have no alternative but to shelf this project indefinitely," the boss assented unhappily.*

Asserted: expressed in a bold or forceful manner in an effort to make one's opinion/s known. Affirmed; contended; declared; emphasized; insisted; maintained; upheld. *"This company was left to me by my father,"* asserted David, *"and no one is going to tell me how to run it."*

Assessed: set or determined the amount, extent, significance or value of. Appraised; estimated; evaluated; valued. *"This diamond is worth millions,"* assessed the jeweler appreciatively.

Assuaged: diminished the intensity or severity of something nasty or unpleasant. Alleviated; appeased; calmed; lessened; pacified; soothed; tempered. *"Hush now, get some rest,"* assuaged mother. *"I will sit right here beside you until the storm has passed."*

Assumed: took for granted. Believed; thought; understood. *"I was under the impression,"* assumed Alan, *"that we had already reached an understanding regarding that issue."*

Assured: stated in a positive, confident way so as to remove doubt. Confirmed; ensured; guaranteed. *"Luckily your daughter's injuries were quite minor. She'll be back on her feet in no time,"* the doctor assured.

Atoned: made amends or reparations for a fault or sin. Compensated; repented. *"I'm sorry I let you down, sis,"* atoned the eldest brother. *"It won't happen again."*

Attacked: criticized strongly or hostilely. Set upon violently or forcibly. Assailed; assaulted; blamed; disparaged; impugned. *"It was you!"* attacked Sh'ryn angrily. *"You stole the Serpent's Eye from the temple!"*

Attempted: made an effort at something. Endeavored; strove; tackled; tried; undertook; ventured. *"Please,"* attempted the tearful young woman, *"if you'll just let me explain everything I know we can work this out."*

Attested: declared positively to be correct, genuine or true. Gave testimony or bore witness to. Affirmed; confirmed; corroborated; substantiated; swore; testified; verified. *"It was Sean McPhearson I saw leaving the scene of the crime,"* *the eyewitness attested.*

Authorized: granted authority, permission or power to. Approved; commissioned; empowered; permitted; sanctioned; vouched for. *"You can have your search warrant,"* *authorized the judge, "but you had better be right about Jack Carr's involvement in this case."*

Averred: declared positively. Expressed or stated formally as a fact. Affirmed; declared; insisted; justified; maintained; professed. *"No, cousin, I am the true heir to the throne of Shirak,"* *averred Timon.*

Avouched: emphatically or authoritatively stated the provable truth or validity of. Admitted; affirmed; avowed; confessed; confirmed; declared. *"This envelope containing numerous pieces of evidence will prove my client's innocence once and for all,"* *avouched the defense attorney.*

Avowed: admitted the existence, reality or truth of boldly, openly or unashamedly. Admitted; announced; confessed; disclosed; proclaimed; revealed; swore. *"Your general speaks the truth, Andeus, it was I who attempted to end your ruthless reign,"* *avowed Dorin.*

-B b-

Babbled: talked foolishly, idly or incoherently. Blurted out rapidly or indistinctly. Blabbered; chattered; clamored; cooed; murmured; prattled. *"You should have seen her, long red hair in disarray, clothes rumpled, the buttons of her lacy bodice undone,"* *the chambermaid babbled. "I swear the princess looked just like a common harlot."*

Bade: issued a command or order to. Invited or summoned to attend. Directed; instructed; ordained. *"Take this urgent message,"* bade the wounded officer. *"See that General Addams of the third battalion gets it before it's too late."*

Badgered: annoyed, harassed or pestered in a persistent manner. Bullied; goaded; harried; irritated; persecuted; plagued; troubled. *"Come on, mom,"* badgered Katie, *"it's just a rock concert. It's not like I'm leaving the planet or something."*

Baited: enticed with strategy or trickery. Attacked or tormented as with insults or ridicule. Antagonized; badgered; heckled; provoked; teased. *"You're nothing but low life scum too stupid to run this or any operation, Vinnie,"* baited the cop.

Balked: stopped short, refusing obstinately or abruptly to go on. Evaded; hesitated; impeded; refused; resisted. *"I'm not saying another word until I see my lawyer,"* balked the jewel thief.

Bandied: gave and received words in a casual or frivolous manner. Tossed comments, ideas or opinions back and forth. Exchanged; swapped; traded. *"You may be older and stronger, but I'm better looking and much more intelligent,"* bandied one of the twins.

Bantered: spoke to in a good-humored, playful or teasing way. Jested; joked; needled; teased. *"Well, if the truth be known,"* Sally bantered, *"you do sort of resemble the creature from that movie we just saw. But only in a good way."*

Bargained: made an agreement between parties establishing terms to which both parties are bound. Agreed; bartered; pledged; promised. *"I'll give you the information you want,"* bargained Jim, *"but in return, you have to cut a deal for me with the D.A."*

Barked: uttered abruptly in a harsh, loud or sharp voice. Bellowed; roared; shouted; snapped. *"Get out,"* barked the frightened fireman, *"the warehouse is caving in!"*

Bawled: cried or sobbed loudly and vehemently. Reprimanded in a loud or harsh voice. Blubbered; howled; wailed; wept. *"Go to your room, you ungrateful little wretch!" bawled the evil stepmother. "There'll be no dinner on the table for you tonight!"*

Bayed: uttered a deep, prolonged bark or howl. Clamored; bellowed; yelled; yelped. *"Oh, God!" bayed the terrified man. "I've been shot!"*

Beamed: expressed by means of an expansive or radiant smile. Glowed; radiated; shone; smiled. *"His majesty and I wish to thank you for saving our kingdom," beamed the queen appreciatively.*

Beckoned: signaled or summoned through the use of some sort of gesture. Gesticulated; gestured; invited; motioned to; waved to. *"Over here," the reporter beckoned. "I think you'll find the evidence you've been looking for."*

Begged: made an earnest, humble or urgent plea for, or request of. Beseeched; entreated; implored; pleaded; supplicated. *"Please," the girl begged, "if you let me go I promise not to tell a soul."*

Began: took the first step or set into motion. Commenced; initiated; embarked on; started. *"Well," began the old woman slowly, "once upon a time there were three bears."*

Belched: ejected or expelled noisily through the mouth as in an explosive or violent manner. Burped; discharged; erupted; gushed; spouted. *"The king's guard sure was tasty," belched the dragon as he picked his teeth with one sharp talon. "What's for dessert?"*

Belittled: spoken of as being contemptible, unimportant or less than another. Disdained; disparaged; maligned; scorned; sneered at. *"And you have the nerve to call yourself a king, you cringing little coward," belittled the black knight.*

Bellowed: roared deeply in a loud powerful voice. Hollered; shrieked; shouted; whooped; yelled. *"You won't get away with this!" the prisoner bellowed. "The rebels will find me and when they do—"*

Bemoaned: wept over. Expressed grief, pity or regret over. Bewailed; lamented; mourned. *"We've lost everything in the fire, everything!" bemoaned the young woman. "What are we to do now?"*

Berated: criticized, reprimanded or scolded angrily and at length. Chewed out; rebuked; reproved; tongue-lashed; upbraided. *"Young man, how many times do I have to remind you to wash your hands after you've been playing outside," berated mother.*

Blabbered: chattered idly or incessantly. Revealed by talking indiscreetly or without reserve. Babbled; gossiped; jabbered; prattled; yakked. *"Rumor has it that old Hank Pratt is having an affair with a woman young enough to be his granddaughter," blabbered Mrs. Black.*

Blackmailed: threatened to expose a criminal act or indiscretion. Coerced; extorted; forced; shook down; squeezed. *"Do as you are told," blackmailed the crook, "and the police will never know of your involvement with the robbery."*

Blamed: held responsible for something such as a fault, error or offense. Censured; condemned; criticized; faulted; reproached. *"If you had been doing your job instead of sitting in some bar none of this would have happened," blamed the distraught woman.*

Blanched: removed the color from causing to turn white or pale. Bleached; faded; paled; whitened. *"It was awful!" the nurse blanched. "I've never seen so much death and destruction before."*

Blared: uttered or proclaimed in a flamboyant or harsh, noisy manner. Bellowed; blasted; resounded; trumpeted. *"You there!" blared the captain of the guard. "Stop in the name of King Altos."*

Blasphemed: spoke of something revered in an impious or irreverent manner. Cursed; profaned; reviled; swore. *"The ancient gods are useless, impotent beings,"* blasphemed the wise one. *"They care for nothing and no one but themselves."*

Blasted: vigorously attacked or criticized. Assaulted verbally in a violent manner. Bellowed; erupted; exploded; roared; screamed. *"You pathetic old fool,"* Marcus blasted, *"can you not see how your selfishness and greed has destroyed your people?"*

Blazed: flared up suddenly as in anger. Blasted; burst; erupted; exploded. *"I hate you!"* blazed Adrienne, her eyes glowing fiercely. *"I don't ever want to see your face again!"*

Blessed: invoked divine favor or conferred well-being on. Adored; bestowed; glorified; hallowed; honored; venerated. *"Thank you for your kindness,"* blessed the old woman falling to her knees before Darius. *"Our village will have peace and prosperity once more thanks to you."*

Blinked: looked at with feigned innocence, surprise or dismay. Winked quickly as if to hold back or remove tears. *"I'm sure I don't know what you mean,"* Allison blinked, her expression impassive.

Blistered: voiced or disapproved of harshly. Admonished; reproved. *"You're wrong, Talia,"* blistered Shannara, *"but I guess you need to find that out on your own."*

Blubbered: uttered while weeping noisily. Cried; sobbed; wept. *"I can't—I can't believe he's really gone!"* blubbered Suzy as she placed a little wooden cross on Mr. Whisker's grave.

Bluffed: deterred, impressed or mislead by a display of false confidence. Deceived; deluded; duped; faked; fooled; pretended. *"I can get you the money,"* bluffed the FBI agent. *"Let the hostages go and the one million dollars you requested is yours."*

Blundered: uttered foolishly or without thought. Made a serious mistake due to ignorance or confusion. Botched; bungled; erred. *"Oh, no!" blundered Jan. "I've managed to spoil Randy's surprise party on Sunday. The others are going to be furious with me!"*

Blurted: uttered suddenly and impulsively. *"All right, I admit it," the terrorist blurted, "I planted the bomb at the state building. Question is, can you reach it in time?"*

Blushed: became red or rosy in the face as from embarrassment or shame. Flushed; reddened. *"He doesn't even notice me," blushed Tara, "but I love him just the same."*

Blustered: made loud empty threats, or spoke loudly in an arrogant or bullying manner. Boasted; bragged; bullied; swaggered. *"I can beat you blindfolded with one fist tied behind me back," blustered the red faced drunk.*

Boasted: uttered in a self-admiring or prideful manner. Glorified oneself with claims of superiority over others. Bragged; blustered; crowed; flaunted. *"It is a well known fact that I am the greatest lover in all the land," Arthus boasted to his friends.*

Boiled: lost one's temper. Experienced intense agitation. Fumed; raged; seethed; smoldered; stewed. *"It is true what they say," boiled one of the villagers. "None of this would be happening if it wasn't for his foolish pride."*

Booed: an utterance used to express contempt or disapproval, or meant to frighten or surprise. *"Get the bum off the stage," booed the crowd, "and bring out the dancing girls."*

Boomed: made a deep resonant sound. Blasted; roared; rumbled; thundered. *"You there!" the giant boomed as one large hand blocked the little man's path. "If you wish to pass through my land safely you must first pay me a toll."*

Bossed: issued orders arrogantly or in a domineering fashion. Controlled; commanded; ordered; supervised. *"I'm the eldest and when mother isn't here, you'll do as I say,"* bossed Tanya.

Bowed: bent the body, head or knee in consent, courtesy, defeat, greeting or deference to. Acquiesced; capitulated; relented; submitted; succumbed; yielded. *"Your wish is my command, my king,"* bowed the humble servant. *"I will carry out your orders at once."*

Bragged: asserted oneself in an arrogant or boastful manner. Boasted; exaggerated; talked big. *"I'm rich, famous and handsome,"* the young actor bragged, *"I can have any woman I want."*

Brayed: uttered loudly and harshly like the sound of a donkey's cry. *"Remember my words,"* brayed the old hag, *"you will regret the day our paths crossed."*

Breathed: uttered quietly as in a whisper. Permitted to rest and regain one's breath. Drew breath; gasped; murmured; puffed; respired; whispered. *"Lana, it's safe now,"* breathed Ursula, *"you don't have to hide anymore."*

Bribed: gave, offered or promised something in an attempt to corrupt, influence or persuade. *"If you let me go unharmed I'll see that you're well rewarded for your troubles,"* bribed the hostage.

Bridled: expressed anger, scorn or resentment. Took offense at. *"Don't tell me how to raise my children when you've none of your own,"* bridled the father.

Bristled: reacted in anger or defiance. Stood stiffly. Disturbed; ruffled; stiffened; took offense. *"I am so old enough to fight in this war,"* bristled the youth.

Brooded: contemplated moodily and persistently. Fretted; moped; sulked; stewed; worried. *"I can be of no use to the cause as long as I* *remain my enemy's prisoner," brooded the young soldier.*

Bubbled: displayed unchecked or unrestrained activity or emotion. Effervesced; gurgled; sparkled. *"Can you believe it, the king's ball is tonight!" bubbled the pretty young redhead.*

Bullied: treated in an aggressive, intimidating or overbearing fashion. Dominated; frightened; harassed; oppressed; tormented; tyrannized. *"From now on I run things around here. Anyone who doesn't like it can take things up with my man Crunch," bullied the leather clad gang member.*

Burped: expelled gas from the stomach. Belched; discharged; erupted; gushed; spewed; spouted. *"Excellent meal," burped the contented warlord, "now, where is that pretty little slave of mine."*

Burst: came apart or seemed to come apart due to overwhelming emotion. Gave sudden expression to; emerged or came forth in a sudden emotional outbreak or outburst. Erupted; exploded; gushed forth; spouted. *"Santa's here, Santa's here!" burst Caitlin as she ran to the window.*

Bustled: moved about energetically and busily. Dashed; fluttered; fussed; hurried; scrambled; scurried. *"Oh, there's no time for that now, princess," the old maid bustled. "We must hurry, the ball is about to begin at any moment."*

Buzzed: uttered excitedly or rapidly in a low or droning voice. Droned; hummed; murmured; whispered. *"Have you heard?" buzzed Marcy. "One of the band members is expected to make an unscheduled appearance at the club tonight."*

-C c-

Cackled: laughed or talked in a piercing, high-pitched tone. Chattered foolishly. *"You'll find out soon enough what happens to those who defy the gods,"* the old woman cackled.

Cajoled: persuaded gently and repeatedly with appeals, flattery, teasing or false promises. Beguiled; coaxed; enticed; sweet talked; wheedled. *"If you do this one small thing for me,"* cajoled Trish, *"I'll do whatever you want me to tonight."*

Calculated: estimated the likely outcome. Conjectured; counted on; determined; guessed; reckoned; supposed. *"If we hurry,"* calculated the guide as she stared up at the darkening sky, *"we can reach base camp before the storm hits."*

Called: uttered in a loud voice. Announced; convened; hailed; hollered; summoned. *"Hello,"* Aaron called from the doorway, *"can anybody hear me?"*

Canted: insincere speech full of banal, trite or pious remarks or statements. Spoke or uttered in a singsong manner. Moralized; pleaded; whined. *"Great goddess, Hera, hear me,"* the high priestess canted. *"Accept this sacrifice from your loyal servants as a sign of our devotion."*

Capitulated: surrendered under specified conditions agreed upon in advance. Came to terms with. Acquiesced; gave up; relented; submitted; succumbed; yielded. *"All right, all right, don't shoot,"* capitulated the drug lord, *"I'm throwing out my weapons and coming out unarmed."*

Carped: found fault in a disagreeable manner. Belittled; chided; complained; criticized; disparaged; nagged; reproached. *"In spite of all your efforts you're still a spineless, pathetic excuse for a soldier,"* carped the lieutenant.

Castigated: berated, scolded or reprimanded severely. Chastised; criticized; disciplined; punished; rebuked. *"Your father and I taught you right from wrong," castigated mother. "There is no excuse for the things that you've done."*

Caterwauled: made a shrill, discordant sound like that of a cat in heat. Argued noisily; rent the air. Clamored; howled; screeched; shrieked. *"Stop! Noooooo," caterwauled the hideous creature as it melted into a lifeless gray mass at the children's feet.*

Caviled: raised trivial objections. Found frivolous or unnecessary fault with or flaws in. Carped; derided; disparaged; quibbled. *"I cannot possibly be expected to marry him," the queen caviled arrogantly, "his eyes are much too close together and his lips are too thin."*

Celebrated: observed with appropriate festivity, rejoicing or respect. Exalted; extolled; honored; praised; proclaimed. *"Let there be music and dancing," celebrated Lord Dansbury, "for today we have won our independence from Merrick the Mighty."*

Censured: criticized strongly or harshly. Admonished; blamed; condemned; disapproved of; rebuked; reprimanded. *"You have left me no choice but to send such willful and disobedient children as you to bed without supper," censured the nanny.*

Certified: confirmed formally as accurate, genuine or true, or as meeting a particular standard. Approved; attested; authenticated; substantiated; validated; verified. *"The test results indicate the presence of a toxic substance in the blood of the dead man," Dr. Stevens certified solemnly.*

Challenged: acted or stated in defiance. Demanded an explanation, justification, proof or validity of the accuracy, truth or genuineness of. Dared; defied; disputed; questioned. *"You dare call yourself a king. You have no more right to be king of Tiber than common barnyard fowl," challenged Sir Ralph.*

Championed: defended another or a cause with extreme enthusiasm, fervor or passion. Aided; advocated; backed; promoted; supported; upheld. *"Our lives are yours, my queen," championed the centurion. "My soldiers and I will do whatever is necessary to ensure your safety."*

Chanted: uttered in a monotonous, rhythmic manner. Crooned; intoned; sang; trolled. *"Murderer! Murderer!" chanted the angry crowd as the prisoner was led to the gallows.*

Charged: instructed or urged with authority. Made a claim of wrongdoing against or held responsible for. Made a violent attack against. Accused; attributed; blamed; commanded; directed; indicted; instructed. *"Although you may not have actually pulled the trigger, you are as guilty as if you had," Sergeant O'Reilly charged vehemently.*

Chastised: punished or criticized severely. Disciplined; penalized; rebuked; reprimanded; scolded. *"For staying out past your curfew your mother and I have decided to ground you for a month," chastised father.*

Chatted: conversed in a casual, easy, familiar or informal manner. Chattered; gabbed; prattled. *"Oh, the party was wonderful," Wendy chatted happily. "I only wish you could have been there."*

Chattered: talked idly, incessantly or rapidly about trivial matters. Made short, rapid, inarticulate sounds. Babbled; blabbed; jabbered; prattled. *"The stranger was tall and dark with long wavy brown hair and as handsome as the day is long," chattered Natasha.*

Checked: acted, spoke or influenced in such a way as to stop the motion or expression of. Constrained; curbed; rebuffed; rebuked; restrained; suppressed. *"Not another word," checked aunt Emma shaking her head sadly, "you've told enough lies for one day, young man."*

Cheered: shouted with approval, encouragement, enthusiasm or joy. Acclaimed; congratulated; delighted; hoorayed. *"Long live the king! Long live the queen!" the crowd cheered noisily.*

Chided: scolded mildly or voiced mild disapproval in an effort to correct or improve. Admonished; berated; criticized; denounced; reprimanded. *"I am very disappointed in your test scores," the teacher chided. "We both know that you are capable of doing so much better."*

Chimed: interrupted the speech of another with an unsolicited comment or opinion. Agreed with or was in harmony with. Accorded; harmonized. *"Dinner and a late movie sounds good to me," chimed Brittany.*

Choked: had difficulty breathing, speaking or swallowing due to emotion, constriction or obstruction of the throat. Gagged; held back; repressed; stifled; suppressed. *"You!" choked Tom, his face livid with barely suppressed rage. "I'll kill you for what you did to my wife!"*

Chortled: laughed or chuckled with a joyful snort in satisfaction or exultation. Chuckled; clucked; guffawed; snickered; sniggered; tittered. *"Not bad sword play . . . for a girl," chortled Simon.*

Chuckled: laughed quietly or to oneself. Chortled; clucked; guffawed; snickered; sniggered; tittered. *"Kids," uncle Ken chuckled, his eyes sparkling, "sometimes they really do say the darndest things."*

Cited: mentioned or quoted in an effort to illustrate, prove or support a belief, opinion, etc. Honored or commended formally or officially. Alluded to; indicated; praised. *"The Bible says, 'judge not lest ye be judged,'" cited the convict.*

Clacked: chattered rapidly and at great length in a thoughtless manner. Prattled; talked idly. *"Back in the good old days children were seen and not heard. Back then, they had respect for their elders," the old* *blind man clacked nostalgically.*

Claimed: stated as factual or true especially when open to question or challenge. Demanded as rightfully belonging to or due oneself. Asserted; called for; maintained; professed; required. *"I provided the map and the transportation, therefore, the bulk of the treasure belongs to me," claimed the captain of the ship.*

Clamored: complained, demanded or protested insistently, vigorously and noisily. Bellowed; blustered; cried out; shouted. *"No new taxes! No new taxes!" clamored the belligerent crowd.*

Clapped: struck together, especially the palms of the hands, resulting in a sharp, explosive sound. Applauded; cuffed; hit; swatted; thumped. *"Bravo!" clapped Mary Beth as she rose to her feet with the others.*

Clarified: removed confusion or uncertainty; made easier to comprehend. Cleared up; elucidated; explained; made understandable. *"The best way to remember those bones is to think of the 'femur' as being closer to the 'feet', and the 'humerus' as being closer to the 'head,'" Trent clarified.*

Clowned: entertained with antics, jokes or tricks. Cut up; jested; kidded around. *"Look at me," clowned the boy in an attempt to cheer up his friends. "I can stand on my head and drink milk at the same time."*

Coached: gave instruction. Directed; drilled; instructed; taught; tutored. *"With a few minor revisions," coached Mr. Daniels, "your speech is sure to win first prize."*

Coaxed: persuaded or influenced another through the use of persistent flattery, pleading or gentle urging. Cajoled; sweet-talked; wheedled. *"If you want to stay home I'll understand, but I'd really rather have my beautiful, charming wife by my side when they announce my promotion at the party tonight," Stan coaxed sweetly.*

Coddled: gave in to another's desires and whims. Babied; gratified; humored; indulged; pampered; spoiled. *"Of course you can have double fudge cake for dessert," coddled the kind old nanny.*

Coerced: controlled, dominated or restrained through the use of force, intimidation or threats. Bullied; compelled; constrained; threatened. *"You will never see your family again if you don't do exactly as I say," coerced the kidnapper.*

Comforted: offered strength and hope to in times of distress or trouble. Calmed; consoled; eased; reassured; soothed. *"Everything will be just fine," comforted Joanna. "Now close your eyes and get some rest."*

Commanded: issued orders with authority. Bid; directed; instructed; ordered; ruled. *"The four of you go around the back and mount an attack from the rear," the officer commanded. "The rest of you come with me."*

Commandeered: took forcibly or arbitrarily. Appropriated; seized; took. *"I'll be taking that gun now, Mr. Johnson," commandeered the policeman.*

Commemorated: paid homage or tribute to; honored the memory of. Celebrated; hailed; memorialized; revered. *"On this day we remember those heroes who gave their lives in the service of their country," commemorated the mayor.*

Commenced: entered into. Began; embarked on; initiated; started. *"My fellow Americans," commenced the vice-president slowly, "this is indeed a sad day for us all."*

Commended: represented someone or something as desirable, worthy or qualified. Approved of; endorsed; lauded; praised; recommended; supported. *"My boys gave it their all the entire season. They deserve this trophy," commended coach Martin.*

Commented: expressed a personal reaction or attitude about something or someone. Annotated; clarified; elucidated; reflected; remarked. *"No, I don't feel what those men did was justified,"* the *mother of five commented to the reporter.*

Commissioned: authorized or empowered to perform specific duties or tasks. Appointed; assigned; charged; delegated; mandated. *"The royal seal will see you safely into foreign lands. Go now,"* commissioned *his majesty, "take this message to King Tyreus before it is too late."*

Communed: communicated intimately with. Was in a state of heightened sensitivity and receptivity. Conferred; conversed; parlayed. *"Oh, great Goddess of the Earth, as always I am thankful for your bounty,"* communed Ti'ra as she fell to her knees before the altar.*

Communicated: expressed oneself in a clear and easily understood manner. Conveyed; disclosed; informed; notified. *"It is important that you pay close attention and take good notes or your lack of diligence will be obvious come test time,"* communicated the teacher patiently.*

Compared: noted the similarities or differences between. Contrasted; equated; likened. *"This vase has a much more intricate pattern than that one,"* compared Vicki with a scrutinizing eye.*

Compelled: drove, exerted or urged through the use of strong physical force, or moral or social pressure. Constrained; exacted; necessitated: pressured; swayed. *"You will return the gem to the people to whom it belongs,"* compelled the hero, "or I will return it for you."*

Competed: rivaled another or others to attain a goal or prize. Contended; fought; opposed; vied. *"You had better be fast on your feet today,"* competed Donna as she warmed up at the starting line, *"because I plan on taking home the ribbon for first place."*

Complained: expressed feelings of dissatisfaction, resentment, grief or pain. Found fault; griped; grumbled; whined. *"She always gets the* *good parts," Melissa complained miserably. "Maybe I should throw myself at the director like she does."*

Complimented: expressed admiration, affection, congratulation, praise or respect. Commended; flattered; honored; lauded; saluted. *"Y–you look incredible tonight, Jessica," complimented Alex shyly.*

Complied: adapted one's actions, speech or thoughts to conform with another's request, rule or wish. Abided by; adhered; conformed; deferred; gave in; yielded. *"We will give you one day as you requested," complied the chief, "but after that we attack our enemy."*

Compromised: made concessions in an attempt to settle differences. Agreed; bargained; made a deal; settled. *"All right. We'll go see a movie tonight," compromised Sid, "but tomorrow we go fishing."*

Computed: determined or calculated by mathematical means or the use of a computer. Ascertained; figured out; reckoned; tallied; totaled. *"As you can see from my figures," computed the confident executive, "the company will be running in the black in less than a month."*

Conceded: grudgingly admitted to be just, proper or true. Allowed; granted; relinquished; surrendered; yielded. *"The voters have spoken and you've won fair and square. It was a good race, Harold," the republican candidate conceded with a handshake.*

Concluded: arrived at after careful deliberation, reasoning or convincing evidence. Decided; deduced; determined; gathered; inferred; surmised. *"And that," the detective concluded with a flourish, "is how I was able to determine that the butler was the mastermind behind the thefts."*

Concurred: expressed a like opinion. Agreed; assented; coincided; cooperated; matched. *"The princess is right. The only way to save the castle is to retreat now and live to fight another day," concurred the captain of the guard.*

Condemned: expressed strong disapproval of. Pronounced a harsh judgment against. Convicted; criticized; denounced; judged; sentenced. *"For your crimes against his majesty and the people of Osha you are to be banished from this land forever," condemned the magistrate.*

Condescended: lowered oneself to an inferior level. Dealt with another or others in a superior or patronizing manner. Deigned; descended; disdained; patronized; stooped. *"Cyril always knows best," the rich old widow condescended, "what with his Ph.D. from a state university and all."*

Conferred: gave or granted publicly. Compared views. Accorded; awarded; bestowed upon; consulted; conversed; discussed. *"For the services you have rendered this land you shall henceforth be known as the Peace Bringer," conferred High Lord Zandor.*

Confessed: made known something damaging or inconvenient to oneself. Acknowledged; admitted; disclosed; divulged; exposed. *"It's all true," Annette confessed tearfully. "I paid someone to tamper with your wife's brakes to prevent her from coming between us."*

Confided: told something to another or others confidentially, privately or secretly. Disclosed; divulged; entrusted; imparted. *"If you promise to go straight to bed I'll tell you a very special story that only a few people are privileged enough to know," confided uncle Mac in a hushed voice.*

Confirmed: established or supported the truth or validity of. Authenticated; corroborated; substantiated; validated; verified. *"The remains found in the wreckage were those of your husband and two children," confirmed the police detective quietly. "I'm sorry."*

Confronted: came up against in a defiant or hostile manner. Challenged; dared; defied; opposed; withstood. *"Who are you to tell me what I can and can't do when the two of you smoke like chimneys and drink as if there's no tomorrow," confronted Tina angrily.*

Congratulated: expressed joy over or acknowledged another's achievements, good fortune, happiness or success. Complimented; felicitated; hailed; rejoiced with; saluted. *"You're a lucky man, Billy," congratulated dad. "Karen will make a fine wife."*

Conjectured: arrived at based on inadequate evidence or guesswork. Deduced; guessed; hypothesized; inferred; speculated; surmised. *"Gentlemen, I believe that what we saw last night was a genuine spaceship from another planet," Hal conjectured, his voice taut with excitement.*

Conjured: summoned by incantation or invocation. Influenced with magical or supernatural power. Beseeched; bewitched; charmed; evoked; invoked. *"Great sorcerer Sousa, grant me the power to crush my enemies beneath my feet," conjured the old witch as she danced around the fire.*

Connived: feigned ignorance of, failed to prevent, or cooperated secretly in a wrongful act. Colluded; conspired; plotted; schemed. *"Listen, you have to believe me," connived Laverne, "I had no idea Damien planned on robbing that convenient store."*

Consented: agreed to another's course of action, opinion or proposal. Allowed; assented; concurred; endorsed; sanctioned. *"All right," consented mother after much discussion, "you can go out with Andre on a school night, just be home by ten."*

Considered: reached after careful thought or deliberation. Took into account. Appraised; contemplated; gauged; pondered; reflected on; weighed. *"Hmmmmmm," the boss considered for a long moment, "you may very well have found the solution to our problem, Ms. Kingston."*

Consoled: lessened the distress, grief or suffering of. Comforted; cheered; eased; soothed; sustained. *"Sleep now. Things will be better in the morning," consoled mother. "I promise."*

Conspired: planned or plotted secretly to commit an unlawful or wrongful act. Colluded; connived; contrived; schemed. *"At exactly 3:30 tomorrow afternoon," conspired the terrorist gleefully, "New York city will cease to exist."*

Contemplated: looked at attentively and thoughtfully. Considered carefully and at length. Examined; inspected; meditated; mulled over; pondered; ruminated; weighed. *"I like your idea, however . . ." contemplated Charles with a frown, ". . . I believe there are still a few bugs that need to be worked out before the board will approve your plan."*

Contended: strove in opposition or rivalry, or against difficulties. Competed with another. Argued; debated; disputed; maintained; struggled; vied. *"I'm the best choice for CEO of this company," Frank contended heatedly, "and we both know it."*

Continued: resumed a train of thought, action, etc. after an interruption. Carried on; endured; lasted; persisted; persevered. *"As I was saying," continued Marge with a sidelong glance at her partner, "I feel our best option is to sell while we still can."*

Contradicted: asserted or expressed an opposing view. Countered; denied; disputed; opposed; refuted. *"The queen had nothing to do with the king's death," contradicted Talos loudly. "It is his majesty's eldest son who is responsible for the loss of our beloved ruler."*

Contributed: gave or supplied along with others. Helped bring about. Advanced; conferred; forwarded; influenced; presented. *"And I can make my famous apple pie for the picnic," aunt Lily contributed cheerfully.*

Contrived: formulated a plan with cleverness, ingenuity or evil intent. Devised; concocted; managed; plotted; schemed. *"I will find a way to take the throne," contrived Sebastian, "even if it means ridding the world of the last descendants of Phyton."*

Conversed: expressed feelings, ideas, opinions or thoughts verbally. Chatted; spoke; talked. *"As you can see,"* conversed Shannon confidently, *"our company has carefully weighed all the options."*

Conveyed: communicated or made known. Confided to; disclosed; divulged; imparted; related; told. *"I have the information you requested on Mr. Jansen,"* conveyed Miss Sommers.

Cooed: talked fondly or amorously in whispers. Uttered in soft, murmuring tones. *"Hush now, child,"* Martha cooed soothingly. *"Time for you to close your eyes and go to sleep."*

Corrected: made free of error or fault. Made or set right what was wrong. Amended; rectified; remedied; revised. *"That is not what I said,"* mother corrected patiently. *"I said you could stay over Darla's house IF you finished your chores."*

Corroborated: strengthened or supported with evidence or authority; made more certain. Authenticated; backed; confirmed; substantiated; validated. *"Julia is telling the truth. I know, because she was with me at the time of the murder,"* corroborated Ted.

Coughed: expelled air from the lungs with a short, noisy burst or bursts. *"Please,"* coughed the old man, his face contorted with pain, *"promise me you'll take care of Anna after I'm gone."*

Counseled: gave advice or guidance often as a result of a consultation. Advised; guided; recommended; suggested. *"With the surgery your chances for a long healthy life are excellent,"* Dr. Clancy counseled.

Countered: acted or responded in a contrary or defiant manner. Contradicted; opposed; retaliated. *"I'm the leader of this rebellion,"* countered General Zarko. *"We do this my way or not at all."*

Courted: attempted to gain the affections, favor or love of through attention and/or flattery. Incurred; invited; pandered to; sought; wooed.

"Tell me, my sweet Melina, that you will marry me," courted Tyrone, "and make me the happiest man in all of Cimmaron."

Craved: had an intense desire or begged earnestly for. Hoped, hungered, longed, pined, thirsted, wished or yearned for. Coveted; implored; lusted after. *"Please, oh, please," craved Fran, "let me have just one more piece of that delicious milk chocolate."*

Cried: shed tears due to grief, pain or sorrow. Uttered loudly; sounded an alarm. Called out; sobbed; shouted; wailed; warned; wept; whimpered. *"Guards! Guards!" cried the boy. "The prisoners are trying to escape!"*

Cringed: shrank from as in fear, or behaved in a servile manner. Cowered; fawned; flinched; groveled. *"Forgive me, master," cringed the haggard old slave. "Give me one last chance to prove my loyalty and devotion to you."*

Criticized: found fault with. Judged the merits and shortcomings of. Disapproved of; disparaged; evaluated; nit-picked; reproached. *"You are a lazy, good-for-nothing drunkard, Thomas Eastman, and I won't put up with your sorry ways another minute," criticized aunt Belle crossly.*

Croaked: uttered in a low, hoarse voice. *"Is anybody there? Can anybody hear me?" croaked the injured climber from the narrow ledge.*

Crooned: hummed or sang softly or in a low voice. *"Sleep, sweet babe. Sleep the whole night through," Alice crooned as she rocked the young child slowly back and forth in the overstuffed chair.*

Cross-examined: questioned closely regarding answers or information given previously. Examined; grilled; probed; queried. *"Tell us once more in your own words, where were you on the night of August fifteenth?" cross-examined the attorney calmly.*

Crowed: made a loud, shrill sound. Exulted loudly as over another's defeat. Boasted; bragged; exulted; gloated; swaggered. *"Yes!" Tamara crowed triumphantly, "I've beaten you for the third time in a row! Care to try again?"*

Cued: prompted another's actions or speech. Gave information or instruction. Hinted; prompted; signaled; tipped. *"Ahem! You were saying—" cued Brandon helpfully.*

Cursed: invoked evil or misfortune on someone or something. Blasphemed; cussed; damned; swore. *"From this day forth everyone who casts their eyes upon you will run from you in horror," cursed the evil wizard.*

-D d-

Damned: pronounced harsh or adverse judgment on. Condemned to punishment for all eternity. Blasted; cursed; doomed. *"Your soul will rot in Tartarus until the end of time," damned the young maiden.*

Dared: challenged or confronted boldly. Bet; defied; provoked; ventured. *"Fight me, mighty Drakor," Jareth dared loud enough for the others to hear, "and if you win, all that I have is yours."*

Debated: considered thoughtfully. Argued, discussed or disputed a question or issue. Deliberated; pondered; reflected; thought about. *"I do not agree, as the king insists, that war is the only answer," Sir Ulrich debated.*

Decided: settled on without doubt or question; made up one's mind. Arrived at a verdict. Chose; concluded; decreed; determined; resolved. *"The festival will go on as planned," decided the high priest despite the encroaching storm clouds.*

Declaimed: spoke loudly and vehemently. Vented angry disapproval. Uttered aloud in a rhetorical manner. Orated; pontificated; railed; sermonized. *"We will not allow ourselves to be dissuaded from our destiny,"* declaimed the rebel commander before the cheering troops.

Declared: stated authoritatively or emphatically, often in the face of potential contradiction. Made known in a formal or official manner. Affirmed; asserted; proclaimed; professed. *"Today will long be remembered as the day that Sparta reclaimed its freedom,"* Luther declared victoriously.

Declined: expressed polite refusal. Failed to accept. Balked at; rejected; spurned; turned down. *"I am afraid that I will be unable to accept your hospitality, your majesty,"* declined Nathan with a bow, *"but I thank you for the generous offer of your lovely daugher just the same."*

Decreed: pronounced, ordered and enforced by law or a court. Commanded; dictated; mandated; proclaimed. *"You, Lord Darth, have been convicted of treason and are sentenced to death tomorrow at dawn,"* the chief elder decreed.

Decried: belittled, condemned or disapproved of openly. Criticized; denounced; disparaged. *"The wizard is a pathetic charlatan,"* decried Sarai loudly. *"He is using your belief in his powers to further his own evil plans."*

Deduced: reached a conclusion through the use of reason. Inferred from a general principle. Comprehended; gathered; reasoned. *"It was Paul who left the unsigned note which led the police to arrest Zachary for the murder of Miss Watkins,"* deduced the detective with a flourish.

Deemed: had an opinion. Believed; considered; judged; regarded; thought; viewed. *"Regardless of bloodlines, Andrew is the only true heir to the king's throne,"* deemed Sir Edward.

Defamed: damaged another's character or reputation through false or malicious statements or writings. Spoke ill of. Discredited; libeled; maligned; slandered. *"That woman is nothing but a murdering adulteress," defamed the next door neighbor. "She got exactly what she deserved."*

Defended: kept safe from attack, danger or harm. Championed; guarded; protected; shielded; upheld. *"I won't let you hurt them," defended Lando, waving his sword bravely before the fire-breathing dragon.*

Deferred: submitted to another out of respect or recognition of authority. Acceded; capitulated; obeyed; submitted; yielded. *"As you wish, Sire," the magician deferred, bowing as he left the courtyard.*

Defied: opposed, resisted or refused to submit with boldness and assurance. Stood up to. Challenged; confronted; disdained; spurned; withstood. *"I will do no such thing, Father," defied Princess Leanna, "and there is nothing you can say or do to change my mind."*

Delighted: took great pleasure or joy in. Was amused, charmed, enchanted or pleased. Enjoyed. *"Oh, you should have been there," delighted the Contessa. "The evening was absolute magic."*

Demanded: requested urgently or insistently. Commanded; exacted; insisted upon; required. *"Where were you until 3:30 this morning?" mother demanded, arms folded tightly across her chest.*

Demurred: voiced opposition or took exception to. Disagreed; objected; protested. *"If you want my honest opinion," demurred Cindy angrily, "your plan sucks!"*

Denied: refused to acknowledge, allow, believe, grant or recognize. Contradicted; disavowed; refuted; rejected. *"What you said about Todd isn't so," denied Adrienne vehemently. "He's simply not capable of committing such a heinous crime."*

Denigrated: verbally attacked the character or reputation of. Badmouthed; belittled; defamed; disparaged; maligned; slandered. *"You are nothing but a self-centered, power-hungry old hag who cares for no one but herself," denigrated Sharon before the entire committee.*

Denounced: condemned openly as being evil or reprehensible. Accused; censured; criticized; vilified. *"This girl is a witch and she must burn at the stake for her sins against God and country," denounced the bishop of Aquila.*

Depicted: described or represented with words. Chronicled; detailed; dramatized; portrayed; recounted; related. *"It was a stormy night, the sort that even the most seasoned sailors dread," depicted Captain Brody, his eyes glowing darkly in the firelight.*

Deplored: expressed strong disapproval of, or sorrow or grief over. Bemoaned; censured; condemned; lamented; mourned; regretted. *"Oh, my God, what have I done!" Jackie deplored miserably.*

Deprecated: expressed disapproval of. Belittled; denigrated; deplored; depreciated. *"I don't want you hanging around with that Johnson girl. She's nothing but trouble," deprecated mother.*

Derided: laughed at or spoke of scornfully or with contemptuous mirth. Mocked; ridiculed; scorned; sneered at. *"So, they've sent their great and powerful Avenger to bring me in, dead or alive," derided Dr. Blackheart. "Catch me, if you think you can, superhero!"*

Described: gave an account of or conveyed ideas, impressions or thoughts in speech or writing. Characterized; depicted; detailed; explained; portrayed; related. *"The night air was cool and sweet, the sky filled with a million twinkling stars," described Jenna dreamily.*

Designated: indicated or specified. Appointed or selected for a special purpose such as an office or a duty. Allocated; chose; named; pointed out. *"Sergeant, take four men and cover the back of the warehouse,"* Lt. Thompson designated brusquely. *"The rest of you come with me."*

Desired: expressed a longing, wish or request for. Coveted; craved; hungered for; wished for; yearned for. *"I don't care about riches or power. All I want,"* desired Sabrina with all her heart, *"is to go home."*

Despaired: was overcome by a sense of futility or defeat; lost heart or faith in; had no hope. *"Oh, Sissy, they'll never find us in this storm,"* despaired Lucy. *"We're doomed to freeze to death in the middle of nowhere."*

Despised: regarded with contempt, scorn or intense dislike. Abhorred; detested; disdained; loathed; scorned. *"You are an evil, twisted man and I will never submit to your will,"* despised Princess Kasha.

Determined: decided or settled an issue conclusively and with authority. Ascertained; concluded; decided; discovered; established; learned; resolved. *"All the lab tests are in. Congratulations, you are cancer free,"* Dr. Hunter determined with a smile.

Diagnosed: identified a disease from signs and symptoms. Analyzed; examined; investigated; studied. *"What you have is a simple case of the flu,"* diagnosed Dr. Adams.

Dictated: said or read aloud for the purpose of being recorded or written down by another. Issued commands or orders with authority. Decreed; imposed; mandated; ordered; pronounced. *"You there, take this message to General LaSalle as fast as your horse can carry you,"* dictated Captain Gregory.

Differed: was dissimilar in thoughts or opinions. Took issue with. Contrasted; disagreed; disputed; dissented. *"Blanche thinks that the centerpieces should consist of chrysanthemums. I think we should use carnations,"* differed Megan.

Digressed: strayed from the main point or subject in speech or writings. Went off on a tangent. Diverged; deviated; strayed; swerved. *"Speaking of sports," digressed Brian, "when I was a kid one of my favorite things to do was go fishing with dad."*

Directed: took charge of. Indicated, pointed out or showed the way. Issued authoritative instructions to. Commanded; guided; instructed; led; ordered; managed; supervised. *"Everyone move behind the yellow line now," officer Fletcher directed impatiently.*

Disagreed: was dissimilar in thought or opinion. Had a dispute or quarrel with. Clashed; deviated; differed; opposed. *"But I feel the red dress is more appropriate for the party," disagreed Gloria.*

Disallowed: refused to admit or recognize. Rejected as improper, invalid or untrue. *"My husband would never cheat on me," Ingrid disallowed vehemently.*

Disapproved: refused approval or had an unfavorable opinion of. Criticized; denounced; disparaged; frowned upon; objected to; vetoed. *"I can't believe you went against my wishes and pierced your nose anyway," mother disapproved sadly.*

Disavowed: denied or renounced any knowledge of, responsibility for or connection with. Abjured; denounced; disowned; recanted; rejected; repudiated. *"I am not now, nor have I ever been, a member of a Nazi organization," the general disavowed heatedly.*

Disbelieved: held not to be real or true; refused to believe in. Was skeptical. Distrusted; doubted; mistrusted. *"You'll never convince me that my brother was a traitor," disbelieved Olivia.*

Disclaimed: denied or renounced any claim to, connection with or the validity of. Abnegated; denied; disaffirmed; disavowed; renounced. *"My company has never been involved in illegal campaign contributions," disclaimed the CEO.*

Disclosed: made known that which was secret. Broadcast; exposed; divulged; revealed; told. *"Have you heard that Edgar is having an affair with Millie?" disclosed the secretary.*

Discounted: reduced in value. Omitted from an account as untrustworthy. Minimized the significance of. Regarded another's words doubtfully. *"I wouldn't put much stock in what he says," discounted Robert. "He thinks he knows everything."*

Discriminated: made a clear distinction between by noting the differences. Made sensible or wise decisions. Differentiated; disdained; judged; separated. *"This computer seems to have more of what we're looking for in the way of memory and speed for the price than than the one we saw earlier," discriminated Wesley.*

Discussed: carefully considered the pros and cons of. Considered; debated; examined; parleyed. *"Multiple choice questions seem to be preferred by students, but the answer is either right or wrong, giving the student all the points or none. Whereas essay questions generally allow one to get at least a few points even on questions they may be unsure of," discussed the professor with a colleague.*

Disdained: regarded with aloofness and haughty contempt. Abhorred; despised; detested; loathed; scorned; snubbed. *"He is such a boring individual," the young lady disdained, "I hope he doesn't plan on speaking to me."*

Dismissed: refused to accept or recognize. Sent away or directed to leave. Adjourned; discharged; discarded; disregarded; released. *"I've heard enough of your backtalk, Rusty," dismissed father, "now go to your room."*

Disobeyed: failed or refused to follow a command, order or rule. Refused to submit to. Countered; defied; disregarded; rebelled against; resisted; transgressed. *"No, sir," disobeyed the soldier, "I will not arrest those civilians."*

Disparaged: spoke of in a degrading or slighting manner. Lowered in esteem, rank or reputation. Belittled; demeaned; depreciated; mocked; ridiculed; slighted. *"What is wrong with you, Lance? Don't you have any brains in your head?" disparaged the coach.*

Dispatched: moved or performed with speed. Sent off to a specific destination. Put to death. Executed; expedited; forwarded; hastened; slayed; transmitted. *"Detective Grant, you and your partner are to take the witness to our most secure safehouse," dispatched the Chief of Police.*

Disproved: proved to be in error, false or invalid. Controverted; discredited; refuted. *"These documents refute your claim that this particular work of art is a forgery," disproved the curator.*

Disputed: questioned the truth or validity of. Engaged in a verbal controversy. Quarreled angrily or heatedly. Argued; challenged; contested; contradicted; debated; doubted; squabbled. *"The Boston Red Sox were not the winners of the 1954 World Series," disputed the sports announcer. "From my recollection, they weren't even in that series."*

Disregarded: paid no attention or heed to. Treated as unworthy of notice or without proper respect. Ignored; neglected; overlooked; slighted. *"Throw those filthy peasants into the dungeon," disregarded the king haughtily.*

Dissented: had a difference of opinion or sentiment. Withheld one's approval or assent. Differed; disagreed; objected; opposed; protested. *"Well I think the smaller car is the best one to buy," dissented Barry.*

Dissuaded: used persuasion or urged strongly to deter from some course of action or purpose. Advised against; discouraged. *"I wouldn't take that over the counter medicine if I were you," the pharmacist dissuaded. "There have been several complaints recently of adverse reactions to it."*

Distracted: drew another's attention or thoughts away from their original focus. Stirred up or confused with conflicting emotions or motives. Agitated; bewildered; disturbed; diverted; troubled; unsettled. *"Look! Over there," distracted Madge while the girls made a run for it.*

Diverged: departed from the norm; turned aside from a set course or path. Differed in manner, opinionor thought. Deviated; differed; digressed; split off; swerved. *"In spite of the fact that I am a conservative Republican, I plan on voting for this legislation," diverged the Senator.*

Diverted: turned from one course or direction to another. Distracted another from their worries or cares. Amused; deflected; distracted; entertained; sidetracked. *"Here's a nice red, cherry lollipop for you, Abby," diverted the nurse as she quickly gave the little girl her vaccination.*

Divined: discovered or perceived by inspiration, intuition or reflection. Forecast; foretold; predicted; prophesied; surmised. *"I see wonderful things happening to you in the near future," the psychic divined.*

Divulged: made known that which was private or secret. Disclosed; imparted; revealed; told. *"The boss is going to layoff ten people during the next month," Dana divulged to her co-workers.*

Documented: supported a change, claim, statement, etc. with evidence or information. Backed up; certified; substantiated; supported; verified. *"Approximately $2,000,000 worth of jewelry was stolen from the store according to Mr. Weaver's records," the insurance investigator documented.*

Dodged: evaded a question or obligation through cunning, deceit or trickery. Avoided, ducked; eluded; hedged; sidestepped. *"I'm sorry, we seem to be out of time, I'll address that issue during the next press conference," dodged the presidential nominee.*

Dominated: exerted strong authority, control, mastery or power over. Controlled; domineered; governed; ruled. *"From now on you WILL do as I say, WHEN I say,"* dominated Zelda over the young man kneeling at her feet.

Doted: showed excessive affection, fondness or love for. Fussed over; lavished. *"You will now and forever be the one and only love of my life,"* doted Gary as he gazed deeply into Pam's pretty blue eyes.

Doubted: was uncertain or skeptical about the reality, truth or validity of. Lacked conviction. Disbelieved; distrusted; mistrusted; questioned; suspected; wondered. *"Are you sure the recipe calls for four eggs and not two,"* doubted Aunt Betty.

Drafted: selected one or more individuals from a group for compulsory service. Inducted. *"You there in the back, and you with the beard and red cloak,"* drafted the blue knight. *"You men have just volunteered to be soldiers in the king's new army."*

Drawled: uttered with lengthened or drawn-out vowels. *"Oooh, he is sooo cute,"* drawled the teenaged girl as she stared at the handsome young lifeguard.

Dreaded: anticipated with alarm, distaste, fear or reluctance. Feared strongly that which one is powerless to avoid. Cowered at; cringed at; shrunk from. *"But there will be over one thousand people in the audience,"* dreaded Carla. *"What if I make a mistake?"*

Dreamt: conceived of, concocted or invented. Had an ardent desire or deep aspiration for. Desired; fantasized; hoped; imagined; mused; wished. *"Someday I will be the leader of this nation and eventually I will rule the world,"* dreamt the young prince.

Drilled: instructed or trained through the use of repetition as a means of perfecting a skill or procedure. Exercised. *"All you soldiers, run this track ten times, and I mean NOW!"* drilled the Major.

Driveled: spoke in a childish, foolish or senseless manner. Let saliva or spittle flow from the mouth. Babbled; dribbled; drooled; rambled; slobbered. *"Momma, momma," Amber driveled, "lemme see, lemme see, lemme see the new baby."*

Droned: made or spoke with a low dull monotonous buzzing or humming sound. Buzzed; hummed; murmured; vibrated; whirred. *"If Ronald Curtis makes this thirty foot putt, he will be within one stroke of the leader," droned the sportscaster.*

Drooled: spoke in a childish, foolish or senseless manner. Let saliva or spittle flow from the mouth. Showed extravagant appreciation or desire for. Babbled; dribbled; driveled; rambled; slobbered. *"Come here, my little pretty," drooled the toothless old hag.*

Dubbed: conferred an honor or title (such as knighthood) upon. *"Ladies and gentlemen of the court, I give you, Sir Tristan of Brighton," dubbed the king.*

-E e-

Eased: lessened the discomfort, pain, pressure or stress of. Alleviated; assuaged; calmed; comforted; consoled; quieted; soothed. *"Everything will be all right, you'll see," eased the paramedic as she gently squeezed the trapped woman's hand. "I'll stay right here with you."*

Echoed: imitated or repeated another's mannerisms, words, style of dress, etc. Aped; copied; mirrored; paralleled; parroted; reflected. *"Halt, or I'll shoot," echoed Eric as he raised his water pistol at the masked bandit on the television.*

Editorialized: presented an opinion as an objective report. Expressed an opinion in or as if in an article or publication. *"Liberals may have* *a difficult time maintaining their majority rule in the House of Representatives in the coming election," editorialized the reporter.*

Effervesced: exhibited high spirits or excitement. Was animated; was bubbly; was exuberant; was irrepressible; was vivacious. *"I won! I won first prize," Robin effervesced as she ran toward her parents.*

Elaborated: expressed at greater length or in greater detail. Clarified; embellished; expanded; specified. *"Furthermore," elaborated the tour guide, "this statue was not only hand carved, but the bronze from which it was made was imported from France and arrived here by boat in 1874."*

Elbowed: cleared a path by jostling or pushing another or others with the elbow. *"Out of my way you fools!" elbowed the old man as he made his way to the front of the crowd."*

Elucidated: made clearer through the use of explanation. Clarified; detailed; explained; expounded; spelled out. *"Which part of NO don't you understand, the N or the O? Put the two together and it means 'not on your life, pal,'" elucidated Heather.*

Embellished: added ornamentation or fictitious details to a story or account. Beautified; decorated; dressed up; enhanced; exaggerated. *"Not only did I go to Europe but while I was there, several handsome young men asked for my hand in marriage," Gina embellished.*

Emphasized: expressed in a forceful manner so as to indicate importance. Accented; iterated; pressed home; stressed; underscored. *"It's not whether you win or lose," emphasized the coach, "it's how you play the game."*

Empowered: invested with official authority or legal power. Authorized; commissioned; delegated; permitted; sanctioned. *"You their, soldier! You will be responsible for guarding the Temple of Darkness," empowered Zephyr.*

Enchanted: cast a spell over. Bewitched; captivated; charmed; entranced; mesmerized. *"From this moment on you will fall madly, hopelessly in love with Zola,"* enchanted the gypsy as she blew magic dust into Ian's eyes.

Encouraged: inspired with confidence, courage or hope. Fostered; heartened; reassured; spurred; supported. *"Now you listen to me, Peter. You have the talent AND the imagination to see this project through,"* encouraged the producer.

Endured: continued despite hardships. Suffered patiently without giving in. Bore; tolerated; weathered; withstood. *"I know you're all hot and tired. So am I,"* endured Althea, *"but we must keep going or we'll never reach safety."*

Enforced: compelled observance of or obedience to. Implemented; imposed; insisted on. *"I don't care if she is a child, she will abide by the laws along with the others,"* enforced the captain of the guard.

Enjoined: directed or imposed with authority and emphasis. Admonished; banned; counseled; forbade; instructed; prohibited. *"As your new sovereign, all who CANNOT or WILL NOT pay taxes are to be executed in the town square at once,"* enjoined Tyr the Terrible.

Ensured: made certain, safe or sure. Clinched; guaranteed; guarded; protected; secured. *"This house has an alarm system that is tops in the market,"* the Realtor ensured. *"You never need to fear being home alone."*

Entertained: gave thought to. Considered; contemplated; mused over; pondered. *"Hmmmm,"* entertained Helen, *"your idea just may be the thing to get us out of this predicament."*

Enthused: showed or expressed great excitement for or interest in. Was exuberant; was passionate. *"That was the most wonderful meal I have ever tasted,"* enthused the businessman.

Enticed: attracted through the arousal of desire or hope. Beguiled; coaxed; lured; persuaded; seduced. *"The Kingdom of the Seven Mountains shall be yours," enticed the sorcerer, "after you see fit to grant me my wish."*

Entranced: put into a trance. Filled with delight or wonder. Bewitched; charmed; enchanted; enthralled; hypnotized; mesmerized. *"You are no longer in control of your actions," entranced the warlock. "From this moment on you will do my bidding and mine alone."*

Entreated: made an earnest request or petition for. Begged; beseeched; implored; pleaded. *"Please don't kill me, my lord," entreated the terrified peasant. "I'll tell you whatever you wish to know."*

Enumerated: counted off or listed by name. Added up; detailed; tabulated; tallied; totaled. *"—Thompson, Jackson, Taylor, Burson, King," enumerated the drill sergeant. "All present and accounted for, Sir."*

Enunciated: uttered carefully and distinctly. Stated in a precise or systematic manner. Announced; articulated; proclaimed; pronounced. *"The rain in Spain stays mainly in the plain," Camille enunciated much to her teacher's delight.*

Envied: experienced discontent and resentment due to the desire to have another's advantages, possessions or qualities. Begrudged; coveted; was jealous of. *"There goes Patricia in her brand new sports car," envied Richard. "I don't know how she can afford it when she makes less money than I do."*

Espoused: took up, supported or was loyal to another's cause. Advocated; adopted; championed; embraced; promoted. *"I am with you, Sir, however the mission turns out," the ensign espoused to his commander.*

Established: proved the truth or validity of beyond doubt. Put to rest any doubts about. Authenticated; confirmed; corroborated; upheld; validated. *"The pilot of the plane was NOT under the influence of drugs or alcohol when the plane crashed," the investigator established.*

Estimated: judged or stated based on one's impressions or rough calculations. Appraised; assessed; believed; conjectured; considered; surmised. *"This house is in excellent condition and in a superb location. I don't expect it to sell for a penny less than $500,000," the realtor estimated with confidence.*

Eulogized: expressed high praise or paid tribute to. Acclaimed; celebrated; complimented; exalted; hailed; lauded. *"Jerome Eugene Washington was a righteous man and a devoted, loving father of four," eulogized the minister.*

Evaded: resorted to cleverness or deceit in order to avoid or escape. Baffled; eluded; foiled; hedged; parried; sidestepped. *"As to your question, I'm afraid I have a plane to catch and don't have the time to address your concerns properly," evaded the politician.*

Evaluated: examined or judged carefully in order to ascertain the value or worth of. Appraised; assessed; estimated; gauged; weighed. *"These statues are very, very old and worth a tremendous amount of money," evaluated the appraiser appreciatively.*

Evoked: called forth or summoned. Called or conjured up. Elicited; induced; invited; provoked; roused; wakened. *"Spirits of Light, I call upon you to enter this earthly realm so that you may free your followers from the Evil One," evoked Anastasia in a loud, steady voice.*

Exacted: demanded and obtained through the use of force or authority. Claimed; extorted; extracted; took; wrested. *"You WILL get down and give me fifty pushups," exacted staff sergeant Tucker.*

Exaggerated: enlarged a fact or statement beyond what is actual or true. Amplified; embellished; magnified; overstated; stretched. *"I was out fishing the other day when I caught the biggest trout ever seen in these waters,"* the old man exaggerated.

Exalted: raised the status of. Glorified; elevated; honored; lauded; praised; venerated. *"You are the Lord Most High, creator of all that we see"* exalted the high priestess. *"Grant us your protection against the barbarian invaders."*

Examined: inquired into carefully. Questioned closely or formally in order to elicit information. Explored; grilled; inspected; interrogated; investigated; scrutinized. *"What an odd stain on your shirt, Carl. Any idea how you got it?"* examined his wife.

Exclaimed: cried or called out suddenly or vehemently. Bellowed; howled; proclaimed; shouted; yelled. *"This is the most wonderful day of my life. I am so happy!"* Diane exclaimed on her wedding day.

Excused: overlooked or made allowance for some slight offense. Granted permission to leave. Absolved; acquitted; forgave; pardoned; released; spared. *"Since you apologized for sassing your mother, I'll let it go this time,"* excused the girl's father, *"but don't let it happen again."*

Exhaled: breathed out. Huffed; panted; puffed. *"This trek up the mountain is really getting to me today,"* exhaled Ernie exhaustedly.

Exhorted: made an urgent appeal; urged through the use of strong argument, admonition or advice. Encouraged; goaded; implored; persuaded; prodded. *"Please, people, please, listen to what Thaddeus is saying,"* exhorted the elder. *"It is very important for our future and the future of our children."*

Exorcised: freed from a maligning influence through the use of commands, incantations or prayers. *"In the all powerful name of God*

the Creator, I command you, evil spirits, to release this poor soul,"
exorcised the priest.

Expanded: spoke at length or in great detail. Amplified; augmented.
"This southern mansion was built in 1775 by Jasper Palmer, a
member of the Virginia Parliament and quite the ladies man,"
expanded the tour guide.

Explained: made clearer or more intelligible that which was not
known or understood. Offered reasons for or a cause of. Clarified;
defined; elucidated; expounded; justified; made plain. *"If you reduce*
fractions before you multiply them, Tony, it will be much easier to
solve the problem," explained the teacher patiently.

Exploded: increased suddenly, noisily and without control. Erupted
with emotion. *"Get out!" exploded Francesca in a fit of rage.*

Exploited: employed selfish or unethical means to obtain a goal. Took
unfair advantage of. Abused; capitalized on; manipulated; misused.
"You know that promotion you were hoping for. It's yours IF you can
manage to steal the Jordan account from our competitor," exploited
the company president.

Exposed: made known the guilt or wrongdoing of. Branded; disclosed;
divulged; revealed; uncovered; unearthed. *"It was Lawrence Grady I*
saw taking the missing paintings from the art gallery," exposed the
security guard. "I'm quite sure of it."

Expounded: gave a detailed, methodical explanation of. Gave a full
account of. Described; elucidated; explained. *"The young girl's nude*
body was found bruised and battered lying face down on the kitchen
floor," expounded Detective Ryan.

Expressed: made one's feelings or opinions known. Put into words.
Communicated; conveyed; declared; divulged; revealed; stated; voiced.
"I don't mean to be a nag, but you did say that you would take me to

the fair today and I really would like to go," expressed Chelsea.

Extolled: praised highly or sang the praises of. Acclaimed; applauded; eulogized; exalted; glorified; lauded. *"Hail Damon! Hail Damon of Avondale, the greatest hunter in all the land," extolled the towns-people as they lifted the young man upon their shoulders.*

Extorted: obtained from another through the use of force, threats or intimidation. Blackmailed; coerced; threatened. *"You will give me the names of all of the people who saw what happened here," Lt. Williams extorted, "or I'll have no choice but to take you downtown and book you myself."*

Extracted: obtained despite another's resistance or unwillingness. Exacted; extricated; gleaned; wrested. *"Thanks for the information, Bernie," extracted the don. "I'm certain the other families will understand your ratting them out."*

Exulted: was extremely jubilant or triumphant. Delighted; rejoiced. *"We won! We won!" exulted the football team after winning the state championship.*

Eyed: looked at attentively or continuously. Watched closely. Observed; regarded; scrutinized; stared at; studied. *"You have grown into quite the beauty, my dear, Arianna," eyed the old gentleman appreciatively.*

-F f-

Fabricated: concocted in order to deceive. Created; contrived; fibbed; invented; lied; made up. *"I climbed Mount McKinley three times so far," fabricated the muscular man. "Next time I plan on going it alone."*

Faked: presented as authentic or genuine. Concocted; falsified; feigned; forged; pretended; simulated; tricked. *"This is a genuine Picasso from a famous gallery in Florence," faked the art dealer.*

Falsified: made untrue or fraudulent statements. Altered; doctored; faked; lied; misrepresented; tampered with. *"I wrote this thesis entirely on my own without any help from fellow students or faculty," falsified the doctoral candidate.*

Faltered: spoke hesitantly as from a loss of confidence or courage. Stammered; vacillated; wavered. *"I–I planned to wrestle the grizzly at the state fair," faltered Hollis, "but I just–I just couldn't do it."*

Fancied: had a capricious notion or whim. Took a liking to. Dreamt of; favored; guessed; imagined; supposed; yearned for. *"That Todd, he really is one sweet young man," fancied Dolly.*

Faulted: blamed, criticized or found error with. Censured; impugned; reproved. *"Your behavior at school today was totally unacceptable," faulted father. "I expect that you will correct that situation tomorrow."*

Fawned: sought another's attention or favor through flattery or servile compliance. *"You are truly the most gracious woman in the world, your majesty," fawned the servant. "That is why I have come to you with my humble request."*

Feared: felt anxious, apprehensive or uneasy in the face of present or imminent danger. Experienced awe or extreme reverence for. Dreaded; shuddered at; trembled at; venerated. *"I can't drive over the bridge, I just can't," Julie feared, "it's too old and rickety."*

Feigned: represented falsely so as to deceive. Concocted; fabricated; invented; pretended; simulated. *"Coach, my shoulder's acting up again," feigned the pitcher after letting another batter score. "Maybe you'd better take me out of the game."*

Feinted: delivered an attack so as to draw attention from a target or one's real purpose. Bluffed; deceived; dodged; tricked. *"Take that, you filthy beast!" feinted the young swordsman as his friends crept past the two-headed monster unnoticed.*

Fidgeted: behaved or moved about nervously or restlessly. Fussed; jerked; squirmed; twitched. *"Honest mom, I didn't take the last piece of cake," fidgeted Adrian nervously.*

Fielded: gave an unrehearsed response to. *"Well, um, well, I can't say for sure being as I haven't had time to properly investigate that issue," fielded Ada.*

Figured: took into consideration. Assessed; believed; calculated; presumed; regarded; supposed. *"You may very well be right about the instability of the structure," figured Josh as he pored over the blueprints of the Hancock building.*

Finessed: handled a delicate situation with diplomacy, skill or tact. Was discreet or savvy. *"Cody will be allowed to play with the train set for one half hour after which it will be Jeffrey's turn to play," finessed the preschool teacher with a satisfied grin.*

Finished: brought to an end. Completed; concluded; ended; stopped; terminated. *"And that, ladies and gentlemen completes this portion of tonight's program," the speaker finished with a bow.*

Fired: uttered or directed rapidly and insistently. Aroused the emotions making one ardent or enthusiastic, angry or annoyed. Animated; excited; incited; ignited; inspired; sparked. *"To the rear march, column left march, company halt!" fired the drill sergeant in a booming voice.*

Fished: sought in a sly or indirect manner. Cast about; groped; hunted; looked about; rummaged; searched. *"So I hear you have a date Saturday night. Anyone I happen to know?" fished Jess.*

Flagged: to signal with or as if with a flag or some similar object. Fell off in vigor. Grew spiritless; languished; signaled to; warned; waved. *"Over here! Hey, Amber, I'm over here,"* flagged her cousin as she ran toward the boarding area.

Flailed: moved about vigorously or erratically. Struck or lashed out in a violent manner. Trashed. *"I HATE it when you talk like that,"* flailed the gang leader.

Flared: experienced an outbreak or intensifying of emotion. Became angry suddenly. Boiled over; erupted; exploded. *"You make me sick, all of you!"* flared the irrational student. *"I hate this place and everything it stands for!"*

Flattered: gratified the vanity of another through the use of excessive, often insincere, compliments in order to gain favor. Adulated; deceived; deluded; lauded; overpraised. *"You are absolutely the best chef this place has ever had. I just don't know what we would do without you,"* flattered the restaurant owner.

Flaunted: exhibited or paraded oneself ostentatiously or shamelessly. Advertised; boasted; showed off; strutted. *"This bikini really shows off my perfect figure, doesn't it, Dennis?"* flaunted Linda.

Flinched: recoiled or winced involuntarily from something painful, surprising or unpleasant. Cowered; cringed; drew back; shrank; started. *"Ouch!"* flinched the baseball player after being hit on the hand by a pitch. *"That really hurt!"*

Flirted: toyed with in a playfully romantic or sexual manner. Dallied; teased. *"Hey, beautiful, what's a sweet thing like you doing here all alone?"* flirted Maurice.

Flouted: expressed contempt for. Insulted; mocked; scorned; spurned; taunted. *"You are by far the most pathetic creature that ever walked upon this planet,"* flouted Ivan.

Flushed: experienced a reddening of the skin, a brief sensation of heat across all or part of the body, or a rush from embarrassment or strong emotion. Blushed; colored; glowed; reddened. *"I'm so embarrassed, I can't believe I actually said that," flushed Sherry.*

Fluttered: moved about rapidly in an excited, nervous or restless fashion. Hurried; pulsated; quivered; shook; stirred; trembled; was flustered. *"Omigosh, look at the time," Kim fluttered. "It's almost seven o'clock and my date will be here any minute to take me to the prom."*

Forbade: refused to allow another to do, say or use something. Banned; commanded against; disallowed; opposed; prohibited. *"Do NOT open your mouth again, young man," Flora forbade, "or you will be sent to your room for the rest of the night!"*

Foretold: told of or described beforehand. Divined; forecast; foresaw; predicted; prophesied. *"I can see a very happy future for you with someone special in your life," foretold the strange dark haired woman at the county fair booth.*

Forgave: refrained from imposing punishment upon. Renounced anger and resentment against for a fault or offense. Absolved; acquitted; excused; exonerated; overlooked; pardoned. *"You seem genuinely apologetic for your crude behavior, so I will excuse it this time," forgave the caring teacher, "but in the future, I expect you to refrain from hitting others."*

Forswore: renounced or repudiated under oath. Denied; disavowed; perjured; recanted; retracted. *"I never said that. I would never say such a thing about another person," forswore the witness.*

Framed: presented false evidence or contrived events so as to falsely incriminate another. *"I have a letter written in Wes Logan's own hand just days before his death implicating Brent and Tracy in the jewelry heist," framed Logan's partner.*

Fretted: moved about in an agitated fashion. Was troubled or vexed. Agonized; brooded; lamented; sulked; worried. *"Oh, no, the sky is getting dark and I still have a good hour and a half ride ahead of me," fretted Patsy.*

Froze: became motionless or immobile as from fear or surprise. Arrested; became paralyzed; halted; stiffened. *"Oh, my God! I can't believe it's really you," froze the grieving widow. "The authorities told me you died in that plane crash."*

Frolicked: behaved in a carefree, playful and uninhibited fashion. Engaged in gaiety, merrymaking, joking or teasing. Acted up; cavorted; had a ball; romped. *"Come on, aunt Zola, dance with me," her nephew frolicked as he grabbed her hand, pulling her onto the dance floor.*

Frowned: wrinkled the brow in disapproval, displeasure, distaste or deep thought. Glared; glowered; mused; pondered; scowled. *"That was not amusing, young man," frowned the minister. "I will not tolerate that sort of behavior in my church again."*

Fumed: felt or expressed resentment or vexation. Lost one's temper. Exploded; raged; ranted; raved; seethed. *"Why must you persist in doing things your father and I have warned you time and again not to do?" fumed mother.*

Fussed: engaged in useless activity or was needlessly nervous. Was troubled or overly concerned with unimportant matters. Complained; fidgeted; fretted; objected; protested; quibbled; worried. *"Oh, this knitting is just not turning out right at all," fussed Mildred, "No matter how hard I try, I keep missing a stitch."*

-G g-

Gabbed: talked idly or incessantly about trivial matters. Babbled; blathered; chatted; chattered; jabbered; prattled. *"And then I went to the grocery store then to the hat store. "You should have seen all the hats there. They were really busy but I managed to find one I liked anyway," gabbed Connie happily.*

Gagged: experienced a regurgitative spasm in the throat. Choked; heaved; retched. *"I don't feel very well. I think the milk may have been expired," gagged Lester.*

Gambled: took a chance on an uncertain outcome in the hope of gaining something advantageous or beneficial. Engaged in reckless or hazardous behavior. Bet; risked; tempted fortune; wagered. *"I'll take numbers 14, 19 and 20 on the red," gambled Lisa at the roulette wheel.*

Gaped: stared openmouthed in wonder or astonishment. Regarded with awe. Gawked; gazed; ogled; peered; stared stupidly. *"Oh, my God! I have never seen anything so–so breathtaking . . . so absolutely beautiful in all my life," gaped Kirstie as she stepped off the Grand Canyon tour bus.*

Gasped: drew in one's breath sharply as from shock or surprise. Gulped; panted; puffed; spoke breathlessly; wheezed. *"You scared the heck out of me," gasped the startled woman.*

Gauged: determined, evaluated or judged the contents or possibility of. Appraised; ascertained; assessed; calculated; guessed; estimated. *"This could be an antique worth hundreds of dollars," gauged the garage sale customer.*

Gawked: Looked with astonishment. Stared in a dazed or stunned manner. Gaped; gazed; stared stupidly. *"I can't believe it, look over there, I think it's that famous French model!" gawked Kirk.*

Gazed: fixed one's eyes upon intently and steadily. Contemplated; regarded; scrutinized; studied; watched. *"That husband and wife figure skating team is gliding so gracefully across the ice. I just can't stop watching them," gazed Joyce with admiration.*

Gestured: motioned with a part of the body as a means of emphasizing speech. Motioned; nodded; nudged; signaled; waved; winked. *"Hey, Joel, come on over here and sit down with us," the couple gestured to their friend in the crowded restaurant.*

Gibbered: engaged in foolish or unintelligible talk. Babbled; blabbed; chattered; gabbed; prattled. *"Sister Susie Sally sells seashells down by the seashore," the little girl gibbered to her doll.*

Giggled: laughed with repeated short spasmodic sounds. Laughed in a silly or nervous way. Cackled; chuckled; sniggered; tittered. *"I thought that he was talking to me," giggled the starstruck woman.*

Glanced: moved the eyes rapidly from one focus to another. Gave a brief cursory look. Glimpsed; peeked; scanned. *"You and your friend here," glanced the judge sternly, "should both be ashamed of yourselves."*

Glared: fixed one's eyes upon angrily or fiercely. Stared at with a piercing look. Glowered; scowled. *"I am so upset with you right now that I could spit nails," glared the disgruntled customer.*

Gloated: expressed malicious pleasure or self-satisfaction. Basked; bragged; crowed over; reveled in; swaggered; triumphed. *"I became the youngest head of a battalion when I was a mere 16 years old," the decorated officer gloated.*

Glowed: experienced a warm feeling as of pleasure or well-being. Was exuberant or radiant. Blushed; flushed; reddened; thrilled; tingled. *"Oh, this has been an absolutely sensational honeymoon," glowed the bride. "What a wonderful surprise!"*

Glowered: fixed one's eyes upon angrily or sullenly. Frowned; glared; scowled; sulked. *"If you had done your job right we would have gotten that account,"* glowered the boss. *"Instead, our competitors landed it."*

Goaded: prodded, spurred or urged especially with an object such as a long stick. Drove; incited; spurred. *"Git movin' ya durn mule,"* goaded the old miner impatiently.

Gossiped: spoke of things of a personal, sensational or intimate nature. Engaged in chatty, trivial talk. Meddled; prattled; pried; snooped; spread rumors; tattled. *"Did you hear about the lady across the street?"* Joan gossiped to her mother. *"She has had two children by two different men and is expecting again!"*

Granted: accorded a favor, privilege or right. Allowed; bestowed; conferred; consented to; endowed. *"You may have the final piece of that delicious chocolate cake,"* granted grandmother.

Greeted: saluted or welcomed in a friendly and respectful fashion. Hailed; met; received. *"Hi there, Terry, long time, no see!"* greeted his old Army buddy.

Grieved: felt deep mental anguish, distress or sorrow. Agonized; bemoaned; lamented; mourned; wailed; wept. *"Why did he have to die so young? He had so much to live for,"* grieved the mother of the young man lying in the casket.

Grilled: questioned intently and relentlessly. Asked; cross-examined; interrogated; pumped; queried. *"You took that candy from the store without permission, didn't you? Answer me,"* grilled the little boy's mom.

Grimaced: contorted the features in an expression of contempt, disgust or pain. Glowered; scowled; smirked. *"Could you hurry up and get this trunk off of my foot?"* Mike grimaced in pain.

Grinned: drew back the lips exposing the teeth in amusement or mirth. Beamed; smiled; smirked. *"My, aren't you a sight for sore eyes?" grinned Ben as his girlfriend approached the car.*

Griped: complained in a nagging or petulant fashion. Bellyached; found fault; grumbled; muttered; protested; whined. *"Why didn't you wash the dishes? Couldn't you see them piled up in the sink?" mother griped to her daughter.*

Groaned: uttered a deep moan of annoyance, grief or pain. Grumbled; moaned; murmured; whimpered; whined. *"This cramp in my leg is killing me," groaned the halfback during a time out. "I don't know if I can go back in the game."*

Groped: searched for or made one's way about blindly or uncertainly. Felt one's way. Fished for; fumbled; probed; ventured. *"Where are you? I can hear you but I can't see you," groped the crew boss through the dust filled mine shaft.*

Groveled: behaved in a servile, demeaning or abject manner as in subservience or humility. Cowered; crawled; cringed; fawned; sniveled. *"Yes, Master, I shall do as you say," groveled Enir.*

Growled: emitted a deep guttural utterance out of anger or surliness. Grumbled; grunted; rumbled; snapped; snarled. *"Get back here with those books," growled the headmaster, "and stay seated until I tell you to leave."*

Grumbled: muttered discontentedly. Complained in a surly manner. Chafed; griped; grouched; growled. *"If he tells that story one more time I will just die," grumbled the bored widow to her friend on their double date.*

Grunted: emitted a deep guttural sound as in disgust. Growled; rumbled. *"Uggh, this piece of marble is impossible to sculpt," grunted the artist.*

Guaranteed: assured or promised a particular outcome. Attested; made certain; pledged; stood behind; vouched for. *"This car has only 45,000 miles and will last you a long time," the used car salesman guaranteed. "It's perfect for a young couple like you."*

Guessed: formed an opinion without sufficient information or evidence. Assumed; conjectured; deduced; gathered; supposed; surmised; suspected; ventured. *"I'd like to buy this hat for grandpa for his birthday. I think it's just the right size for him," guessed the freckle-faced little girl.*

Guffawed: laughed heartily and boisterously. Howled; roared; screamed; shouted. *"That was soooo funny, I could just die laughing," guffawed Ada as she watched her favorite comedian perform on stage.*

Guided: indicated or showed the way. Conducted; directed; piloted; steered; ushered. *"If you turn left at the next street then right at the first light, you will find the hotel you're looking for," guided the gas station attendant helpfully.*

Gulped: swallowed eagerly. Swallowed air audibly, often out of nervousness or fear. Choked back; guzzled; swilled; wolfed. *"I, well, um, I was hoping that you would agree to marry me," gulped Kent.*

Gurgled: expressed or pronounced in a broken irregular fashion with a bubbling sound. Babbled; murmured; sputtered. *"Late last night I, uh, saw this bright light in the sky and it, well, uh, I think it may have been a UFO!" gurgled Skip excitedly.*

Gushed: made an effusive display of affection, enthusiasm or sentiment. Emitted a sudden and abundant flow as of tears or words. Chattered; gabbed; flattered excessively; issued; poured out; spouted; talked effusively. *"Oh, this is the absolute best present I could have gotten for my birthday. Thanks so very much everybody," Mollie gushed appreciatively.*

-H h-

Haggled: bargained or argued over something in an attempt to come to an agreement or understanding. Bartered; dickered; disputed; quibbled; squabbled. *"I'd really prefer going to Vegas, but I'll settle for New York IF we stay at a fancy hotel while we're there," Nelson haggled.*

Hailed: called out or shouted in order to gain another's attention. Acclaimed or greeted another enthusiastically. Paid tribute to. Exalted; greeted; honored; saluted; signaled; welcomed. *"Over here, Auntie," hailed her niece at the airport terminal. "It's so good to see you again."*

Harangued: spoke in an impassioned, vehement fashion intended to arouse strong feelings. *"Is everybody happy? I asked, is everybody happy? Well, you should be because ladies and gentlemen, this is the first day of the rest of your lives," harangued the speaker.*

Harassed: irritated or tormented persistently or incessantly with repeated annoyances, demands or threats. Badgered; bullied; harried; hounded; persecuted; pestered; plagued. *"You know the drill. Hand over your lunch, you little nerd," harassed the school bully.*

Harped: talked about something to an excessive and tedious degree. *"Oh, you should have seen him," harped Lynn, "he had the biggest dark brown eyes, the cutest dimples and the sexiest grin. By far, he's the best looking guy I've ever seen."*

Heaved: uttered painfully, wearily or with great effort. Gagged; groaned; moaned; retched; vomited. *"Nurse! Nurse! Is it time for my pain medicine yet?" heaved the injured man.*

Heckled: harassed with objections, questions, or taunting or jeering remarks. Annoyed; badgered; hounded; mocked; needled; provoked. *"You suck, you over the hill hippie! I can't believe I paid good money to come to this concert," heckled the drunken fan.*

Hedged: avoided responding to statements or questions in a clear, direct manner. Dodged; ducked; evaded; hemmed. *"I did kind of see what happened, but I'm not sure because I wasn't up close. It could have been him, but then again, I really didn't see the man very well,"* the witness hedged.

Held: maintained one's opinion or position in a given situation. Withstood opposition, pressure or stress. Formally affirmed or asserted. Agreed with or supported. Adhered to; believed; professed. *"I firmly believe that the Bible is the the only true word of God,"* held the minister.

Helped: offered assistance or relief. Aided; backed; eased; furthered; promoted; rescued; supported. *"If you do it this way,"* helped the carpenter, *"you might get the work done quicker and with less effort on your part."*

Hemmed: hesitated or was indecisive in speech. Cleared the throat or coughed in order to fill a pause while speaking, gain attention, hide embarrassment, or warn another. *"Honey, um, I would, uh, well, I need to, um, tell you something important,"* hemmed the newly married woman.

Heralded: made an official or royal proclamation. Announced; divulged; informed; reported. *"From this day forth,"* heralded the King, *"this land shall be known as Victorianna."*

Hesitated: paused in the midst of acting, deciding or speaking due to reluctance or uncertainty. Spoke haltingly. Balked; delayed; faltered; vacillated; wavered. *"Can I . . ."* hesitated Tammy, *". . . can I ask you a personal question?"*

Hiccupped or hicoughed: experienced a spasm of the diaphragm in which the glottis closes suddenly resulting in a sharp, distinctive sound. *"I think I drank my soda a little too quickly,"* hiccupped the teenager.

Hinted: stated in a covert or indirect fashion so as to be understood. Alluded; implied; insinuated; intimated; suggested. *"Those chocolate chip cookies you're baking sure do smell good, mom," hinted Jay, giving the older woman a big hug.*

Hissed: expressed condemnation, dissatisfaction, disapproval or contempt through a sharp sound similar to a sustained "s" or "sh". *"Shhhhhhhhh, be still while you are in the presence of the Master," hissed the kung fu expert.*

Hollered: called out loudly. Bellowed; shouted; yelled. *"Hey, Ref, YOU SUCK, GET SOME GLASSES!" hollered the irate fan.*

Hooted: uttered a loud, raucous cry of contempt, derision or scorn. Shouted down or drove off with jeers. Booed; hissed; jeered; mocked; snickered; taunted. *"Get off of the stage!" hooted the rock fans at the opening act. "We want Jet, we want Jet!"*

Hounded: pursued enthusiastically, persistently or relentlessly. Annoyed; baited; bedeviled; harried; harassed; nagged; pestered. *"Yesterday you promised to help me clean the garage, Alexandra," the frustrated husband hounded. "You promised and I expect you to keep your word."*

Howled: cried out loudly with a long, mournful, plaintive sound as in pain or despair. Laughed heartily; roared with laughter. Bayed; clamored; wailed; yelped; yowled. *"Isn't he the funniest comic you ever heard?" Phillip howled, gripping his sides in pain.*

Huffed: made empty threats against. Reacted with indignation. Took offense. Blustered; raged. *"How dare you say such a thing about my little Darcy," huffed the irate mother.*

Humphed: uttered a sound of contempt, displeasure or doubt. *"Well, I never—" humphed the rich old woman, as she sauntered haughtily from the department store.*

Hushed: made silent or still. Calmed; quelled; quieted; soothed. *"Shhh, my little angel, momma's here and everything will be okay," hushed the young mother as she rocked the crying child to sleep.*

Hustled: urged to proceed with haste. Hastened; hurried; jostled; nudged; prodded; rushed. *"Keep moving, class, we must reach the tornado shelter before the storm hits," hustled the schoolteacher.*

-I i-

Identified: established the characteristics, identity, nature or origin of. Determined; distinguished; picked out; verified. *"That's the man," identified the terrified woman. "He's the one who robbed that store."*

Illuminated: made understandable, or provided intellectual or spiritual enlightenment. Clarified; elucidated; explained; made clear; spelled out. *"When handling yourself, use your head. When handling others, use your heart," illuminated the nursing instructor.*

Illustrated: clarified through the use of comparisons or examples. Demonstrated; emphasized; explained. *"If you will please look at the screen above you, you will see two diagrams which indicate the number of violent versus nonviolent crimes committed in this county during the past five years," illustrated the police officer.*

Imagined: formed a mental picture. Conceived of; conjectured; dreamt up; envisioned; visualized. *"France at this time of the year is supposed to be splendid. Oh, I can just see myself walking along the Champs Elysees," imagined Phoebe.*

Imitated: copied the actions, appearance, mannerisms, speech or style of. Aped; impersonated; mimicked; mirrored; parroted. *"Quack, quack!" imitated the toddler as he crouched by the edge of the pond.*

Imparted: made something known or granted a share of. Bestowed; confided; disclosed; divulged; gave; mentioned; revealed. *"Ned should know how much I love him after all of the things I've done for him,"* imparted Goldie.

Implicated: connected another intimately with. Embroiled; ensnared; entangled; incriminated; involved. *"Well, I wasn't there but I did overhear her saying that she saw what happened the night Dylan's was robbed,"* implicated Frances.

Implied: expressed or indicated in an indirect fashion. Entailed; hinted; inferred; suggested. *"That style of dress would look really nice on someone with a slender figure like yours,"* implied Kurt sheepishly.

Implored: made a humble or earnest appeal. Begged for urgently. Beseeched; entreated; pleaded. *"Please, won't you take the children into consideration when you talk to each other like that,"* the social worker implored.

Imposed: established or applied as compulsory or as by authority. Dictated; levied; placed on. *"There will now be taxes on all items including food and drink,"* imposed the city council.

Improvised: composed, orated, recited or sang without any prior preparation. Ad-libbed; concocted; devised; invented. *"Mary had a little lamb and boy, were the doctors surprised,"* the comedian improvised.

Impugned: opposed or attacked as false or questionable. Assailed; challenged; contradicted; denied; negated. *"That is NOT how the fight got started at all,"* impugned the athlete. *"We were both just goofing around and it got out of hand."*

Incited: provoked or moved to action. Agitated; inflamed; instigated; roused; spurred on; stirred up; urged on. *"Come on, you yellow-*

bellied chicken," incited the class bully. "Or are you too afraid to stand up for yourself, you little wimp?"

Incriminated: accused another of a crime, fault or wrongdoing. Caused to appear guilty. Blamed; charged. *"Yesterday afternoon I saw Mrs. Roper getting very cozy with young Buddy Drake," incriminated the elderly neighbor.*

Indicated: pointed out or showed the way. Directed attention to. Expressed or stated briefly. Dictated; revealed; specified. *"There are emergency exits located in several places along the aircraft," the stewardess indicated in a cursory fashion.*

Indicted: accused formally of a wrongdoing. Arraigned; charged; prosecuted. *"William Taylor, you are under arrest for the rape and murder of Ruby Quinn," indicted the homicide detective.*

Inferred: concluded from evidence, facts or premises. Reasoned from circumstances. Concluded; gathered; gleaned; guessed; reasoned; supposed; surmised. *"After hearing both sides, it seems to me that neither of you is without blame and you should both be sent to your rooms without dessert," inferred father.*

Informed: disclosed confidential or incriminating information to an authority so as to accuse or cast suspicion on. Disclosed information or made aware of. Appraised; notified; squealed; snitched; tattled; told. *"The class trip will be to Niagara Falls this year," Daisy informed her mother.*

Inhaled: drew into the lungs by breathing in. Breathed in; inspired; respired; sniffed; sucked in. *"Oh, Preston," inhaled Eliza, "I never thought I would hear you say those words to me again."*

Inquired: sought information by asking about. Explored; investigated; queried; questioned; probed. *"When was the last time you saw your granddaughter?" the waitress inquired amiably.*

Insinuated: introduced or conveyed gradually and insidiously, or in a subtle, indirect or covert way. Alluded; hinted; implied; intimated; suggested. *"You know, I could've sworn I saw someone who looks alot like you hanging around that new punk bar," insinuated Natalie.*

Insisted: asserted or demanded in a vehement or persistent manner. Refused to yield. Claimed; contended; held; maintained; persisted. *"Before you watch another moment of television you are to finish your homework and take out the trash," insisted mother, hands on hips.*

Inspired: filled with exalting emotion or motivation. Aroused; excited; induced; prompted; stirred; stimulated. *"You can lose all the weight you want and tone up those flabby muscles at the same time with this incredible new gym system," inspired the infomercial guru.*

Instigated: goaded or urged forward. Incited; initiated; provoked; roused; set in motion; stirred up. *"Go ahead and do it, Hector, hit him," instigated his younger brother.*

Instructed: provided knowledge or gave orders. Advised; coached; commanded; directed; drilled; educated; taught; trained. *"In order to throw the ball correctly you need to be sure to hold it the way I showed you earlier," instructed the baseball pitching coach.*

Insulted: treated with gross insensitivity, insolence or rudeness with the intent of humiliating, arousing anger or wounding another's feelings. Affronted; belittled; derided; offended; slighted. *"You are a mean, hateful, unruly little brat and I don't want you hanging around my little Nora anymore," insulted the irate mother.*

Interceded: begged or pleaded on another's behalf. Offered support or help, or put in a good word for. Arbitrated; interposed; intervened; mediated; stepped in. *"This young lady heads her class in math and is one of the top students in science. I think she would do well at your university," interceded the student advisor.*

Interjected: inserted between or among other things. Interposed; interrupted. *"Now, listen here,"* the referee interjected, *"you two men need to settle down so that this game can resume."*

Interpreted: explained the meaning of or offered an explanation. Clarified; deciphered; expounded; made clear; reworded; translated. *"When a woman says NO, then that is exactly what she means,"* interpreted Harlan to the drunken man.

Interrogated: examined or questioned formally. Asked; cross-examined, examined; questioned; probed. *"Sir, did you actually see the defendant running from the scene of the crime?"* interrogated the defense attorney.

Interrupted: hindered or stopped the actions or discourse of another by breaking in on. Obstructed the course of. Halted; interfered with; severed. *"Excuse me,"* interrupted the gentleman apologetically, *"would you be so kind as to repeat your last statement? I'm afraid I couldn't hear you."*

Intervened: to interfere with or come between two things so as to alter, hinder or settle something. Arbitrated; mediated; interceded; interrupted; intruded. *"This strike has gone on long enough,"* Gene intervened, *"I want both parties to start negotiations right now."*

Intimated: made known subtly and indirectly. Alluded; hinted; implied; indicated; suggested. *"A nice cold one would sure feel good on a hot day like today,"* her husband intimated pleasantly.

Intoned: uttered in a monotonous or singsong fashion. Spoke in musical or prolonged tones. Chanted; crooned; drawled; hummed. *"Cleveland rocks! Cleveland rocks!"* intoned the crowd at the dedication of the Rock-N-Roll Hall of Fame.

Introduced: presented someone by name to another or others. Presented another to the public for the first time. Caused to become acquainted. Brought forward a plan or idea. *"This is my daughter, April,"* introduced her mother, *"the one who is still single."*

Invited: politely requested another's presence or participation in. Enticed, provoked or tempted another to say or do something. *"There will be a party in the gym after the last bell rings today, and you are all welcome to attend,"* invited the class president.

Invoked: appealed to a higher power for assistance, inspiration or support. Called for earnestly. Summoned with incantations. Beseeched; entreated; implored; petitioned; prayed for. *"Goddess of Heaven and Earth, grant your humble servants a bountiful harvest,"* invoked the high priestess.

Iterated: stated again. Repeated. *"I'm fine, just fine,"* iterated Amos, *"and you.?"*

-J j-

Jabbered: spoke indistinctly, rapidly or unintelligibly. Talked aimlessly or idly. Babbled; blabbered; driveled; gabbed; rambled. *"You should have seen what happened at the ballgame! The players all got into this big fight, then all sorts of fights broke out in the stands,"* jabbered Bertie.

Jeered: spoke or shouted derisively. Heckled; mocked; ridiculed; scorned; taunted. *"This movie sucks!"* jeered the raucous teens as they watched the old black and white film.

Jested: made a playful, witty, sarcastic or ironic remark not meant to be taken seriously. Joked; quipped; teased; wisecracked. *"Hey, fella, your fly is open,"* jested the comic as a large man in a suit made his way to his seat.

Joined: engaged in, enrolled in or entered into. *"Excuse me for interrupting," joined Otis, "but I strongly disagree with you."*

Joked: spoke or acted in a frivolous and facetious manner. Clowned; frolicked; jested; poked fun at; teased. *"Your old dog is so stupid it fell in love with a pair of hushpuppies," Louis joked.*

Joshed: made or exchanged good-humored remarks. Hazed; poked fun at; ridiculed; teased. *"Hey, sexy, wanna go skinny dipping with me," joshed Sylvia.*

Jostled: made one's way or vied for an advantage position by shoving, elbowing or pushing. Bumped; butted; jabbed; poked; prodded. *"Press! Let me through," jostled the reporter at the presidential conference.*

Judged: declared, determined or formed an opinion after careful consideration or deliberation. Concluded; deemed; decided; regarded; resolved. *"I believe this cold medicine will give you more relief from your symptoms with less adverse side affects than the other brand," judged the pharmacist.*

Justified: proved or showed to be just, right or valid. Released from the guilt of sin and declared righteous. Absolved; defended; excused; sanctioned; vindicated. *"As you can clearly see from a statistical analysis of the data, my hypothesis was indeed correct and warrants further study," justified the researcher.*

-K k-

Keened: wailed loudly or wordlessly in regret, sorrow or grief for or about the dead. *"Oh, God, he's dead! He was so young, I can't believe he's really gone!" the old woman keened.*

Kidded: mocked in a playfully teasing fashion. Jested; joshed; mocked; ribbed; teased. *"Hey, shortstuff, would you mind picking that up for me since you're closer to the ground?" kidded Holly.*

-L l-

Labeled: classified, described, designated or identified with a label. Branded; characterized; earmarked; noted. *"From the looks of you, you must be a jock," labeled the high school coach.*

Labored: proceeded with great effort or strove for painstakingly. Suffered from distress or a burden or disadvantage. Dealt with in exhaustive or excessive detail. Agonized; drudged; slaved; struggled; sweated; suffered; toiled. *"I'll get this statue right no matter how long it takes," labored the sculptor.*

Lamented: expressed deep grief, regret or sorrow for or about. Deplored; bewailed; keened; mourned; wailed; whimpered. *"Leslie's left me for another woman," Cynthia lamented tearfully. "I can't believe our marriage is really over."*

Lampooned: ridiculed or satirized a group, institution or person. Made light of. *"I don't know why anyone would want to marry a professional golfer. I mean, who needs someone who gets teed off eighteen times a day," lampooned the comic.*

Languished: was or became downcast, feeble or weak. Lost strength or vigor. Deteriorated; faded; failed; hungered for; longed for; pined for; waned. *"Please, I need something to eat and drink, languished the homeless man, "can you spare some food or money?"*

Lashed: made a scathing verbal attack against. Struck out with force or violence. Berated; castigated; cursed; hammered; goaded; pounded;

reviled. *"You are by far the sorriest excuse for a human being I have ever had the misfortune to hire,"* lashed the store manager. *"You're fired!"*

Lauded: to give praise to. Acclaimed; commended; glorified; extolled. *"Hail, Ceasar!" lauded the crowd as the emperor rode triumphantly through the streets of Rome.*

Laughed: felt or expressed amusement, good humor or triumph. Felt or expressed contempt or derision. Cackled; chortled; guffawed; mocked; scoffed at; snickered. *"You're so funny,"* Wilma, laughed, *"you just crack me up."*

Launched: began a new venture or entered enthusiastically into something such as a speech. Embarked upon; established; initiated; instituted; started. *"I am very happy to announce the opening of our one hundredth store,"* launched the president of the corporation.

Lavished: gave or bestowed in abundance or with extravagance. Showered; squandered. *"This exquisite diamond ring is for you, my love,"* lavished the newly crowned Prince. *"I hope it will be a constant reminder of my devotion to you."*

Leaked: disclosed confidential information without authorization or official sanction. Divulged; made public; revealed. *"I know for a fact that Cal Walker is planning on running for president,"* leaked the press secretary.

Lectured: admonished or reproved earnestly and often at length. Chided; rebuked; reprimanded; scolded; upbraided. *"You, of all people, should know better than to go over the speed limit,"* lectured the chief to the patrolman.

Led: guided or inspired the behavior, conduct, performance or opinion of. Went or was first, acting as a commander, director or guide. Showed the way. *"C'mon, this way everyone,"* led the tour guide.

Leered: looked at with a sidelong glance indicative of sexual desire or sly, malicious intent. Looked at knowingly; ogled; smirked; stared at suggestively. *"Hey, blondie, nice tomatoes you got there," leered the gangster.*

Lessened: made less or reduced the severity of. Made little of. Alleviated; belittled; decreased; diminished; lightened. *"Oh, that little cut is nothing. It'll be healed before you know it," lessened the school nurse.*

Leveled: directed emphatically or forcefully toward another. Brought to an equal level. *"Do you have any idea what could've happened due to your negligence?" leveled the air traffic controller.*

Levied: imposed or collected, such as a tax. Confiscated money or property in accordance with a legal judgment. Assessed; charged; demanded; exacted. *"You owe the government over $10,000 in back taxes," levied the IRS agent.*

Liberated: set free from confinement or oppression. Absolved; delivered; emancipated; extricated; released; unshackled. *"The king has decided to pardon the lot of you. You are all free to go," liberated the jailer.*

Licensed: gave or yielded official or legal permission to or for. Authorized; empowered; endorsed; granted; permitted; sanctioned. *"You are now approved to sell liquor at your establishment," licensed the state liquor board.*

Lied: conveyed or presented false information with the intention of deceiving. Fibbed; misstated; perjured oneself. *"I don't know nothin' 'bout no murder," the hitman lied.*

Likened: mentioned as similar. Compared; drew parallels; matched. *"You and your sister could be mistaken for twins," likened the neighbor.*

Lilted: played, sang or spoke in a lively or cheerfully rhythmic manner. *"Oh, what a lovely day for a parade," lilted the shopkeeper.*

Limited: confined or restricted within set boundaries. Checked; curbed; restrained; specified. *"You may ride your bike, but remember not to go past the playground," limited mother sternly.*

Lingered: was slow in leaving especially out of reluctance. Proceeded in a slow, leisurely or aimless manner. Remained feebly alive for a period of time before dying. Delayed; persisted; procrastinated; tarried. *"I guess I really should be going being as it's late and all," lingered Elliot awkwardly. "Would it be all right if I called you sometime?"*

Liquidated: settled a claim, debt, obligation or affairs of. Put an end to. *"After twenty-five years in the same location Yale Furniture is going out of business," liquidated the owner.*

Lisped: spoke in an imperfect manner and characterized by mispronunciation of *s, z, th* as in thin, and *th* as in this. *"Stop calling me names," lisped the little girl as she ran from the classroom.*

Listed: itemized a series of names, words or other items. Enumerated. *"Let's see, we have tomatoes, cucumbers, lettuce and radishes for the salad," listed the cook.*

Loathed: disliked someone or something intensely. Abhorred; despised; detested; disdained; hated; recoiled from. *"I can't stand liver," loathed Foster. "Do I really have to eat it?"*

Lobbied: tried to influence public officials for or against a specific cause. *"Stop cutting down our rainforests," lobbied the crowd outside the government building.*

Longed: expressed an earnest, heartfelt desire for that which is beyond reach. Aspired; coveted; craved; sought; yearned. *"It would be so great to be lying on the beach right now," longed Erin with a sigh.*

Lurched: staggered or pitched suddenly or erratically. Canted; careened; reeled; stumbled; teetered; tottered. *"G'night, Gil,"* lurched *the drunk as he headed for the door, "see ya tomorrow night."*

Lured: attracted or enticed by wiles or temptation. Allured; beguiled; fascinated; seduced; tantalized. *"Come here, little girl, I have some candy for you,"* lured the kidnapper.

Lusted: expressed an intense or unrestrained sexual craving for. Coveted; desired; hungered for. *"I can hardly wait to be alone with you, my love,"* lusted the new bride. *"Only a few more hours!"*

Luxuriated: indulged oneself or took luxurious pleasure in. Basked; delighted; relished; wallowed in. *"This hot tub feels sooo good on my aching muscles,"* luxuriated Gayle, *"I could stay in it forever."*

-M m-

Maintained: defended against attack or criticism. Declared to be true. Carried on or continued. Affirmed; asserted; claimed; contended; insisted; sustained; upheld. *"The good old U.S. of A., despite all it's flaws, is still the best country in the world to live in,"* the general maintained.

Maligned: uttered evil, harmful and often untrue statements about another. Defamed; disparaged; slandered. *"She's a black witch,"* maligned Hester. *"I've seen her practicing her evil magic with my own eyes."*

Managed: succeeded with difficulty in accomplishing or achieving something. Coped with; dealt with. *"Since Herschel's death things have been difficult financially, but I'm doing all right in spite of the setbacks,"* managed the widow.

Mandated: decreed or required by law. Made mandatory. Commanded; dictated; ordered; sanctioned. *"All citizens of this land must come forth and be counted in the census,"* the king mandated.

Maneuvered: altered one's strategy or changed one's tactics. Manipulated into a desired position or toward a specific goal. Contrived; deployed; plotted; schemed. *"The enemy expects us to try to take that hill so we'll march across the river and secure the bridge instead,"* maneuvered the major.

Manipulated: controlled or influenced to one's advantage by artful, devious or indirect means. Handled; managed; plied; used. *"If you do this, you will not only be helping your people, but you will ensure yourself a place in history,"* manipulated the traitor.

Manufactured: concocted, fabricated or invented. Created; devised; fashioned; made up. *"I can't sleep, mommy, cause there's this big, hairy monster that keeps waking me up,"* manufactured the little boy.

Mapped: planned out in detail. Arranged; delineated; laid out; organized. *"Our vacation will consist of a brief stopover in New York, then a short stay in Boston before we continue on to the Cape,"* mapped father.

Marveled: felt amazement, astonishment, bewilderment or wonder at or about. Was awed. *"Look at the moon, how bright and full it is,"* the young woman marveled.

Masqueraded: had or put on a deceptive appearance or went about as if in disguise. Impersonated. *"I am the Duke of York,"* masqueraded the jewel thief. *"What an honor to be invited to your lovely home."*

Masterminded: directed, planned or supervised something such as an activity or project. Conceived; engineered; organized. *"If we follow my plan, we will be able to take over the majority of shares in this company within six months,"* masterminded the executive.

Meddled: interfered in another's or others' affairs. Handled in an idle or ignorant manner. Intruded; intervened; pried into. *"You really should watch your children more carefully,"* meddled *the elderly neighbor. "One of these days they're going to get run over and it will be your fault."*

Mediated: intervened between conflicting parties in order to bring about an agreement or compromise. Arbitrated; interceded; intervened; negotiated; refereed; settled. *"All right you two, time to stop arguing and start discussing the issue at hand,"* mediated *mother.*

Meditated: considered, contemplated or reflected on at length. Deliberated; mused; pondered; ruminated; thought about. *"I wonder if there really is intelligent life on other planets,"* meditated *Zach.*

Menaced: uttered threats against. Browbeat; bullied; intimidated; terrorized. *"Hey, creep, I think I'll break the neighbor's window with my baseball and blame it on you,"* menaced *the town bully.*

Mentioned: made a casual or incidental reference to. Alluded to; cited; hinted at; implied; insinuated; referred to; touched upon. *"Oh, I know Jarrett Bronson all right. We went to high school together,"* mentioned *Andrea with a grimace.*

Mesmerized: to spellbind. Bewitched; charmed; entranced; enthralled; fascinated; hypnotized. *"Watch the flame closely as you begin to slowly relax,"* mesmerized *Dale.*

Mimicked: copied or imitated another's actions, speech, etc. closely. Copied or imitated so as to mock or ridicule. Aped; echoed; impersonated; mirrored; parroted. *"Stop repeating everything I say,"* mimicked *the unruly child.*

Minced: spoke or acted with affected (artificial) daintiness or elegance. Put on airs. *"Well, we have two vacation homes, one in France and one in California,"* minced *the wealthy teen.*

Minimized: represented as having the least degree of importance or value. *"Ah, that's nothing,"* minimized the ex-marine. *"I've been shot three times in the four years I served my country."*

Mistrusted: regarded with doubt or suspicion. Was wary of. Disbelieved; questioned; suspected. *"Are you sure about that,"* mistrusted the insurance claims agent, *"I heard a completely different version of the same story earlier today?"*

Moaned: uttered a low, sustained mournful cry indicative of grief, pain or sorrow. Bewailed; complained; groaned; keened; lamented; wailed. *"Nurse. Nurse!"* moaned the cancer patient. *"Please, I need more pain medicine."*

Mocked: expressed contempt, ridicule or scorn. Mimicked, as in sport; made fun of. Derided; jeered; reviled; spurned; taunted. *"Hey Queenie, ain't you special you got a car fancier than most people's house?"* mocked the ragged young man lounging on the street corner.

Mollified: calmed or soothed another's temper or feelings. Appeased; assuaged; lessened; pacified; placated; softened. *"Why don't you tell me all about your little spat with Earl over some chocolate chip cookies and a nice cold glass of milk,"* mollified mother.

Monkeyed: behaved in a mischievous or ape-like fashion. Aped; goofed around. *"Look at me! I can swing from tree to tree just like Tarzan,"* monkeyed Glen.

Moped: was dejected or gloomy. Brooded; languished; pined; sulked; worried. *"I can't believe that I haven't received a single job offer since I lost my job four weeks ago,"* Esther moped.

Moralized: expressed moral judgments or explained the moral meaning of. Preached; sermonized; was high-minded. *"Abortion is murder regardless of when it is performed or why,"* moralized the conservative minister.

Motioned: directed or signaled by making a gesture. Beckoned; gesticulated; nodded. *"You kids there, step back behind the yellow line," the Ferris wheel operator motioned.*

Motivated: provided with an incentive or moved to action. Aroused; goaded; influenced; moved; stimulated; stirred. *"Whoever sells the most vacuum cleaners this month will earn an all expenses paid trip to Niagara Falls for the weekend," motivated the sales manager.*

Mourned: expressed deep grief, sorrow or regret for. Bemoaned; cried; despaired; lamented; languished; sobbed; wailed. *"Woe is me, my prince has gone off to war," mourned the pretty maiden.*

Mouthed: expressed one's complaints or opinions in a loud, indiscreet manner. Uttered in an impudent or pompous manner; talked back. Uttered without conviction or understanding. Uttered indistinctly; mumbled. *"I don't have to listen to you," mouthed Hope as she ran to her room. "You're just my father's new wife."*

Mumbled: uttered indistinctly by lowering the voice or partially closing the mouth. Murmured; muttered; rumbled; stammered. *"This teacher sure is boring," Becky mumbled to the girl sitting next to her. "Maybe I should consider changing my major."*

Munched: chewed or ate with pleasure. *"This is delicious," Penelope munched appreciatively, "I think I'll have another helping."*

Murmured: complained in low mumbling tones or uttered in a low, indistinct voice. Droned; grumbled; lamented; mumbled; muttered. *"Durned kids, always running across the grass," murmured the disgruntled old man.*

Mused: uttered after much consideration or thought. Cogitated; contemplated; deliberated; mulled; ruminated. *"I would have to say I prefer Chinese food over Mexican," mused the food connoisseur, "although I like them both."*

Muttered: complained or grumbled morosely. Uttered in low, indistinct tones. Griped; grumbled; mumbled; murmured. *"Got stuck doing the dishes again," Joseph muttered unhappily to himself.*

-N n-

Nagged: annoyed through constant complaining, scolding or urging. Badgered; goaded; harassed; harped; heckled; irritated. *"Doggone it, Alfred, if I've told you once, I've told you a hundred times to put your coffee cup in the sink when you're done," grandmother nagged grandfather.*

Named: mentioned, specified or cited by name. Appointed to, or nominated for a duty, honor or office. Authorized; called; chose; commissioned; delegated; selected. *"Mrs. Timmons will be the new head of the accounting department as of January second," named the boss.*

Narrated: told a story. Gave an account or description of something such as an event. Provided a running commentary for something such as a documentary or performance. Chronicled; detailed; described; portrayed; recounted; related. *"A long, long time ago in a far away land," narrated the story teller, "there lived a wise old man named Jonah."*

Needled: goaded, provoked or teased through speech or action. Hazed; mocked; ragged; taunted. *"Hey, Bif, when ya gonna get a haircut?" needled the gang leader, "You're startin' to look REAL pretty!"*

Negated: made ineffective or invalid; ruled out. Denied; nullified; revoked; squelched; voided. *"The terms of the old contract are no longer acceptable to my client," negated the agent.*

Negotiated: conferred or discussed with another or others in order to come to terms or reach a mutual agreement. Arbitrated; arranged; bargained; contracted; settled. *"If you release the women and children unharmed, we'll send the helicopter as you requested,"* the FBI agent negotiated.

Nibbled: ate with quick bites taking in only a small amount of food at a time. Took small, cautious or gentle bites. Chewed; gnawed; munched; pecked. *"These hors d'oeuvres are simply divine,"* nibbled Genevieve with delight.

Nodded: lowered the head forward slightly and raised it again quickly as a sign of acknowledgment, agreement, command, greeting or invitation. Beckoned; gestured; hailed; recognized; saluted; signaled. *"It is a great honor to meet you, Queen Ophelia,"* nodded the Prince of Valentia.

Nominated: appointed or named to an office, honor, position or responsibility. *"I think that Mr. Patterson would make a wonderful president,"* nominated the treasurer.

Noted: observed carefully; paid close attention to. Made mention of. Denoted or indicated. Heeded; noticed; perceived; remarked. *"I see,"* the doctor noted, *"and exactly when did these symptoms begin?"*

Notified: gave formal notice imparting required or pertinent information. Announced; enlightened; informed; told; warned. *"Space shuttle to earth, space shuttle to earth, we are experiencing some mechanical difficulties,"* notified the commander.

Nudged: gave a gentle push in order to gain another's attention or give a signal. Elbowed; jabbed; poked; shoved. *"Hey, sis, wake up, the show is almost ready to start,"* nudged her brother.

-O o-

Obeyed: submitted to another's control. Carried out or complied with the command, instruction or order of. Acquiesced; concurred; followed orders; heeded; succumbed; yielded. *"Yes, Sir, I will get right on it, Sir," obeyed the sailor.*

Objected: presented a dissenting or opposing argument. Expressed distaste or disapproval of something. Balked; criticized; denounced; revolted. *"But your honor," the attorney objected, "the prosecutor was badgering the witness."*

Observed: said something casually; made a comment or remark. Took notice of. Beheld; declared; discerned; mentioned; opined; viewed; watched. *"There sure are alot of red sports cars on the road tonight," Henry observed.*

Obsessed: was excessively preoccupied with a single emotion, thought or topic. *"Mommy, I just can't go on that elevator, if I do I just know it will get stuck," obsessed the frightened child.*

Obtested: begged for, beseeched, entreated or supplicated. Called as a witness. *"Please, my Lord, do not take all our grain for taxes," obtested the peasant. "The children will go hungry this winter if you do."*

Obtruded: imposed one's ideas or opinions on others with undue insistence or without invitation. Interfered; intruded; meddled; pried. *"The house is lovely, dear, but it would look so much more comfortable if you just arranged a few things differently," obtruded the mother-in-law.*

Offered: presented for consideration. Indicated or expressed one's intention or willingness to do something. Proposed; put forward; rendered; submitted; suggested. *"Let me help you with that bag of groceries, ma'am," offered the young man behind the counter.*

Ogled: stared at in an amorous, flirtatious or impertinent manner. Gaped; gawked; gazed at; scrutinized. *"What a hunk!" ogled Lori as she stared at the handsome actor.*

Opined:held or expressed an opinion. Assumed; presumed; speculated; stated; surmised. *"Trust me Marian, you'll be much better off without that old fool," opined the widow with assurance.*

Opposed: contended or conflicted with in speech or action. Battled; contested; defied; resisted; withstood. *"I will not wear that dress tonight," opposed his wife. "If you like it so much, you wear it!"*

Opted: chose not to continue or participate in something such as a conversation or activity. Picked; preferred; selected. *"I'm really not up to playing poker tonight," opted Roland, "but you can count me in for next week's game."*

Orated: spoke in a bombastic or pompous fashion. Declaimed; harangued; lectured; preached. *"Ladies and gentlemen, come one, come all, to the greatest show on earth," orated the barker.*

Ordained: ordered by virtue of superior authority. Commanded; decreed; dictated; enacted; pronounced; ruled. *"By the power vested in me, I now pronounce you man and wife," ordained the reverend. "You may kiss the bride."*

Ordered: issued a command or instruction to requesting that something be done or supplied. Bade; charged; decreed; directed; enjoined. *"Go to your room and stay there until I call you," the girl's father ordered angrily.*

Organized: brought into being or established. Arranged into a functional, orderly, structured whole. Created; developed; founded; originated. *"While I'm baking cookies dad can bring the Christmas decorations down from the attic and Anna can be in charge of picking out music to decorate by," organized mom.*

Owned: admitted as being in accordance with fact, truth or a claim. Made a full confession. Acclaimed; acknowledged; conceded; concurred; consented; disclosed; recognized. *"Okay, okay, yes, I did it, I took the last piece of cake,"* owned the teen. *"So sue me!"*

-P p-

Paced: walked or strode back and forth across with long deliberate steps. Ambled; plodded; strolled; trudged; walked. *"The suspense is killing me,"* paced the expectant father. *"I don't know how much longer I can take it."*

Pacified: eased another's anger or agitation. Restored calm to. Appeased; mollified; quieted; soothed. *"Everything will be okay, honey,"* pacified the young mother, *"the storm will pass us by soon."*

Painted: described or depicted colorfully or vividly in words. *"The clouds were fluffy and white and the sky a beautiful pale shade of blue the day we spent at Yellowstone,"* painted the happy vacationer.

Paled: became pallid or ashen in complexion. Blanched; whitened. *"Oh, my God,"* paled the spectator, *"that illusion scared me half to death."*

Paltered: spoke or acted in an insincere or misleading fashion. Dealt with facts or decisions lightly or carelessly. Equivocated; quibbled; trifled. *"I see that you've redecorated without consulting me. What an interesting choice of colors,"* paltered the interior designer.

Pampered: gave in to or treated with excessive indulgence. Catered to; coddled; gratified; spoiled. *"Remember the diamond necklace you were admiring the other day? Happy anniversary, honey,"* pampered Yolanda's husband on their tenth wedding anniversary.

Panicked: was affected with a sudden overpowering, often groundless terror. Dreaded; feared. *"No, please don't let the car run out of gas right now,"* panicked the driver as his car began to sputter.

Panted: breathed rapidly in short gasps. Uttered breathlessly or hurriedly. Huffed; puffed; wheezed. *"I can't . . . go much further,"* panted the runner as he staggered toward the finish line.

Paraded: behaved so as to attract attention. Walked about in boastful showiness. Arrayed; displayed; flaunted; showed off; promenaded. *"Do I look good in this crown and dress or what?"* paraded the homecoming queen.

Paralleled: compared ideas, opinions, etc. in order to show likeness or similarity. Correlated; equaled; matched. *"If you look at the charts on the wall, you will see that profits were about the same this quarter as last,"* paralleled the economist.

Paraphrased: reworded the meaning expressed in something spoken or written. Recapitulated; rephrased; restated. *"What he meant was, he really likes you and would like to know if you'd go out with him,"* paraphrased Noel's best friend.

Pardoned: released another from punishment for an offense or exempted from penalty. Absolved; disregarded; excused; exonerated; forgave; overlooked. *"All draft dodgers are now free to return home without fear of prosecution,"* pardoned the president.

Parlayed: bet an original wager and its winnings on a subsequent race, contest, etc. Maneuvered an asset to great advantage. *"I'll bet the $50 I just won plus the minimum wager on Blue Thunder in the third race,"* parlayed the gambler.

Parleyed: had a discussion or conference with an enemy regarding the terms of a truce or the settling of a dispute. Conferred; conversed; talked. *"We will gladly relinquish our rights to the land east of the* *river if you allow us the undisputed right to all the land from here to the west bank,"* parleyed *the king's negotiator.*

Parroted: mechanically repeated the words or actions of others without full understanding. Aped; echoed; imitated; mimed; mimicked. *"Pretty, birdie! Pretty, birdie!"* the toddler parroted *as he stared at the caged parakeets.*

Parried: countered or warded off criticism, a prying question, etc. by a clever or evasive response. Avoided; circumvented; deflected; dodged; ducked; eluded; sidestepped. *"You ask if I've ever cheated on my spouse, well I'm asking you to define cheating,"* parried *the presidential candidate.*

Patronized: was helpful or kind to but in a haughty or condescending manner as if dealing with an inferior. Humored. *"Here let me get that for you. I wouldn't want you to hurt yourself,"* patronized *the stockboy as the elderly woman reached for the canned peaches.*

Pattered: spoke or uttered glibly or rapidly. Recited mechanically or thoughtlessly. Chattered; mumbled; talked meaninglessly. *"Little Miss Muffett, sat on her tuffett, eating her curds and whey,"* pattered *the little girl to her stuffed bear.*

Paused: ceased or suspended action or speech temporarily. Halted; hesitated; lingered; stopped briefly; tarried. *"One moment please,"* paused *the salesclerk as she turned to hang up the phone. "Now, sir, how may I help you?"*

Pecked: criticized or found fault with constantly or repeatedly. Carped. *"You just can't do anything right, can you? You're stupid, stupid, stupid,"* pecked *the stepfather.*

Peeped: spoke in a hesitant, thin, high-pitched voice as from fear. Muttered; twittered; whispered. *"Momma, please hold me,"* peeped *the little girl. "The thunder is so loud."*

Penalized: subjected to a penalty or imposed a handicap on. Placed at a disadvantage. Fined; forfeited; inflicted; punished. *"Encroachment, offense. Mark off five yards,"* penalized the referee. *"First down and fifteen to go."*

Peppered: uttered in a lively and vivid fashion with wit or strong criticism. *"There now! You're just as snug as a bug in a rug,"* peppered the baby-sitter as she tucked the little boy into bed.*

Performed: fulfilled an obligation or requirement, or accomplished something as promised or expected. Attained; carried out; effected; executed; realized. *"Mr. Tate, your letter has been typed and sent out in today's mail as you requested,"* performed the secretary.

Perjured: deliberately testified falsely while under lawful oath. Falsified; fibbed; lied; misrepresented. *"I was at my sister's house the night of the crime,"* the defendant perjured.

Perked: became lively or animated. Regained one's good spirits. *"Did you say that we WILL go to the amusement park after all?"* perked the little girl. *"Yippee!"*

Permitted: allowed another to do or say something. Approved; authorized; condoned; consented; granted leave; sanctioned. *"Since you cleaned your room and did all of your chores, you may go to the baseball game tonight,"* mother permitted.

Persecuted: afflicted or harassed persistently so as to injure or distress. Annoyed; bullied; badgered; bothered; hounded; oppressed; tyrannized. *"I know you're responsible and I'm going to see that you pay for your crimes. Do you hear me, I'm going to make you pay for what you did?"* persecuted Daphne.

Persevered: persisted despite difficulty, discouragement or obstacles. Continued; maintained; was determined. *"I will make it to the top of this mountain, even if it's the last thing I do,"* persevered Stewart.

Persisted: held firmly and steadfastly to a purpose, opinion, thought, etc. despite obstacles, setbacks or warnings. Endured; held on; prevailed; remained; survived. *"I've worked this land for 20 years through droughts and floods and I'm not about to give up now,"* *persisted the farmer.*

Persuaded: induced to do something such as undertake a course of action or embrace a point of view through argument, entreaty or reasoning. Convinced; enticed; motivated; prevailed; prompted. *"Aw come on, honey,"* *persuaded Virginia's fiancee gently,* *"let's go to my folks' house for dinner so they can get to know you better."*

Pestered: annoyed constantly or repeatedly with petty irritations. Badgered; bothered; harassed; taunted; vexed. *"Hey, sissy, can I ride your new bike, can I, please, please, can I?"* *Kelly pestered sweetly.*

Petitioned: asked for or requested formally. Appealed; entreated; invoked; pleaded; urged. *"We really need to get this school levy passed, so please, vote 'yes' on this issue,"* *petitioned Mr. Yates.*

Philosophized: set forth or expressed a moralistic, often superficial love and pursuit of wisdom or knowledge. Idealized; moralized; rationalized; reasoned; theorized. *"The mind is not a vessel to be filled, but a fire to be kindled,"* *philosophized Plutarch.*

Picked: singled out from or recognized among a group. Selected with great care. Criticized sharply or found fault with. Carped; chose; decided upon; nagged; provoked. *"Chief Turner, you will be the new head of the narcotics division,"* *picked the mayor after much deliberation.*

Pictured: described vividly and in detail; made a verbal image of. Depicted; illustrated; portrayed; represented; visualized. *"I can see it now, the rolling waves, the pale blue sky, the warm sandy beaches of Hawaii,"* *pictured Alexis on her wedding day. "I can't wait to step off that plane."*

Pieced: joined or united the individual parts of. Combined; coupled; fused. *"I think this one goes right here," pieced Arnold as he stared intently at the jigsaw puzzle.*

Pinched: squeezed between the thumb and forefinger so as to cause discomfort or pain. Grabbed; nipped; tweaked. *"Stop hitting me," pinched Kay, "or I'm gonna tell mom."*

Pined: had an intense longing or desire. Felt nostalgic. Hungered for; languished; longed; yearned. *"I miss my wife and children so much," the soldier pined. "All I want is to feel their arms around me once more."*

Piped: uttered in a shrill, reedy tone. Spoke up. Cheeped; peeped; trilled; warbled. *"Really? I won the cooking contest?" piped Flo in amazement.*

Piqued: experienced a state of resentment or vexation caused by a perceived slight or indignity. Affronted; aroused; irritated; offended; perturbed; provoked. *"I am very surprised at your rudeness, young man," piqued his uncle. "I thought you had more manners than that."*

Pitied: felt sympathy or sorrow for another's misfortune or suffering. Had compassion for. Commiserated; consoled; empathized. *"Oh, you poor thing, you have a fever," pitied mother.*

Placated: allayed the anger of through the use of concessions. Appeased; mollified; pacified; quieted; soothed. *"Honey, I'm sorry for losing my temper last night. Let me take you out to your favorite restaurant and a movie to make up for it," placated her husband.*

Plagued: annoyed or pestered incessantly or persistently. Afflicted; burdened; distressed; persecuted; troubled. *"You told me you would take me to the beach today, daddy. "So when are we going?" his daughter plagued in a whining tone.*

Planned: devised a program or scheme for the accomplishment or attainment of. Had a specific aim or purpose in mind. Contrived; designed; mapped out; outlined; thought out. *"If we take the back roads we can avoid driving through downtown Chicago at the height of rush hour," planned Michael. "That ought to cut our travel time down by at least an hour or two."*

Pleaded: made an earnest appeal. Offered reasons for or against something. Argued; begged; beseeched; enjoined; petitioned; requested. *"Please, master, please don't punish me," the slave girl pleaded. "I will do whatever you command."*

Pledged: made a solemn binding promise or agreement. Assured; avowed; guaranteed; swore; vowed. *"I, Forrest, do take you as my wife," pledged the groom as he gazed lovingly into his bride's eyes.*

Plied: addressed another urgently or constantly with questions. Assailed; besieged; manipulated; persisted; prevailed upon; wielded. *"I'll ask you once more. Were you or weren't you at the apartment the night of the murder?" plied the lawyer.*

Plodded: moved or walked heavily and laboriously. Drudged; lumbered; paced; shuffled; traipsed; tramped; trudged. *"We're almost there, men," plodded the weary commander as the troops crested the final hill.*

Plotted: formed a secret plan to accomplish a hostile or illegal action. Conspired; contrived; maneuvered; schemed. *"If we make our move at 8:20 we'll have exactly ten minutes before the security guard returns," the burglar plotted. "That will give us plenty of time to clean out the jewelry cases and make our escape undetected."*

Pointed: indicated position or directed attention toward with an object such as a finger, pointer, etc. Brought something to notice or gave emphasis to. Guided; punctuated; steered; stressed. *"The hotel you're looking for is over there," pointed the service station attendant.*

Poked: pushed or jabbed at with a finger or the like. Moved about in a slow, aimless or lazy manner. Ridiculed in a mischievous fashion. Dawdled; elbowed; meandered; nudged; prodded; sauntered; teased. *"Why don't you try thinking for a change before you say something stupid," poked the older sister roughly.*

Policed: maintained order. Controlled; guarded; patrolled; protected, regulated. *"This is Alpha Foxtrot, Sector 12 is secure," policed the sentry on duty.*

Polled: questioned a selected or random group of people to acquire information or determine public opinion. Canvassed; interviewed; sampled; surveyed. *"Which candidate do you think will become the next president?" polled the college student.*

Pondered: reflected upon or considered with thoroughness and care. Contemplated; deliberated; meditated; ruminated; weighed. *"Hmmm, I'm not sure which dress should I buy for the wedding, the pastel pink one or the powder blue one," pondered the bride's mother.*

Pontificated: acted or expressed opinions or judgments in a manner characterized by authoritative, arrogant assertion of unproved or unprovable principles. Blustered; condescended; patronized. *"The death sentence is absolutely wrong, no matter what crime was committed," pontificated the minister.*

Posed: Put forth an argument, claim, etc. Put forward or proposed an idea, question, etc. Set forth in words. Asserted; presented; propounded; submitted; suggested. *"The drought is killing all of the crops, so what are we going to do about it?" posed the farmer at the town meeting.*

Postulated: assumed without proof to be true; took for granted. Made a claim for. Conjectured; demanded; guessed; presumed; surmised. *"I suppose you'll be leaving today, Mr. Russell," postulated the hotel clerk.*

Pouted: uttered or expressed with a show of displeasure or disappointment. Brooded; fretted; moped; scowled; sulked. *The little girl pouted, "I'm not going to go since you said we're not stopping for ice cream on the way."*

Practiced: uttered or performed something habitually or repeatedly in order to learn or perfect a skill. Applied; drilled; exercised; rehearsed; trained. *"Do, re, mi, fa, so, la, ti, do," practiced the singer before her recital.*

Praised: expressed admiration, approval or commendation. Applauded; complimented; exalted; extolled; glorified; lauded. *"After tonight's concert you certainly can call yourself the King of Rock-n-Roll," praised the manager.*

Prattled: spoke in a childish manner. Talked idly or meaninglessly. Babbled; chattered; jabbered; yakked. *"Yabba dabba do, I love you," Nancy prattled to her favorite doll.*

Prayed: made a devout, earnest or fervent request for. Beseeched; implored; petitioned; pleaded; supplicated. *"Oh, God, please let this tornado pass us by," the homeowner prayed quietly.*

Preached: gave moral or religious instruction in a tiresome or tedious manner. Proclaimed or put forth in a sermon. Admonished; advocated; counseled; evangelized; professed. *"You must believe in God and turn away from sin in order to be saved," preached the evangelist.*

Predicted: stated or told about in advance on the basis of special knowledge. Anticipated; envisioned; forecast; foretold; prophesied. *"A wonderful young man will enter your life changing it forever," the gypsy predicted.*

Preened: showed satisfaction with or vanity in oneself. Swelled with pride. Exulted; gloated; primped. *"This dress makes me look totally awesome," preened the high school girl.*

Preferred: liked better. Gave priority or preference to. Chose; fancied; favored; selected. *"I'd rather have a cream filled donut than a glazed one," preferred the officer.*

Prescribed: established or set down guidelines, laws or rules. Ordered the use of medicine or some other form of treatment. Authorized; decreed; dictated; directed; enacted; imposed; specified. *"Take two of these capsules each day for the next two weeks," prescribed the physician.*

Presented: introduced formally to. Offered for consideration, examination or observation. Made a gift or award of. Bestowed; conferred; displayed; exhibited; proposed; put forward; showed. *"And now, I'd like to introduce the valedictorian of the class of 2000, Meredith Hudson," presented the dean.*

Pressed: forced or urged as by insistent or repeated argument. Required haste. Entreated; hounded; impelled; implored; importuned. *"Come on, hurry up Christopher, we're running late," pressed June.*

Pressured: forced as by overpowering influence. Coerced; demanded; hurried; required; urged. *"You know, Matt, we've been engaged for three years now. Don't you think it's about time that we set a wedding date?" pressured his fiancee.*

Presumed: took for granted that something is true or factual lacking proof to the contrary. Assumed; believed; conceived; deduced; supposed; surmised. *"You're much too young to remember the sixties," presumed the elderly lady.*

Pretended: alleged, claimed or professed falsely. Deceived; faked; feigned; imagined; impersonated; masqueraded. *"Yes, sir, I can fix that flat tire in no time at all," pretended the little boy.*

Prevailed: was greater in influence or strength. Produced or achieved the desired effect. Abounded; conquered; overcame; triumphed; was victorious; won out. *"You lose again! I told you I could beat you at arm wrestling,"* prevailed the athlete.

Primed: provided answers, information or instruction beforehand. Briefed; coached; prepared; prompted; readied; trained; tutored. *"Now, repeat after me, xylophone, x-y-l-o-p-h-o-n-e,"* primed the spelling coach.

Primped: dressed or groomed with excessive or meticulous care. Dolled up; preened; prettified; spruced up. *"My hair looks good but I need to comb my beard and straighten my tie,"* primped Oscar.

Prioritized: arranged in order of importance. Ordered. *"I think we should buy the furniture BEFORE we buy curtains,"* the new home owner prioritized.

Probed: examined or investigated with great thoroughness. Delved into; explored; inquired; researched; scrutinized; searched; studied. *"You arrive home three hours late reeking of cologne and have been acting suspicious ever since. Where were you tonight?"* probed the angry wife.

Proceeded: undertook or carried on with some action or speech after an interruption. Commenced; continued; ensued; pressed on; progressed; started. *"As I was saying,"* proceeded the speaker after a cursory look at the disorderly teens, *"this issue is of paramount importance to us all."*

Proclaimed: announced officially and publicly. Advertised; declared; broadcast; heralded; voiced. *"I now pronounce you, Nickolas the fourth, King of Prussia,"* the archbishop proclaimed.

Prodded: goaded or urged into action. Jabbed or poked with some object. Impelled; incited; motivated; prompted; roused; stirred. *"Get going, you old fool, keep it moving,"* the jailer prodded with his nightstick.

Produced: brought to view or offered for inspection. Caused to occur or exist; gave rise to. Brought forth. Created; developed; exhibited; generated; manifested; revealed; unveiled. *"Is this the blouse you were looking for?" produced Tish. "It was in my closet all this time."*

Profaned: treated with contempt or irreverence. Abused; debased; desecrated; mocked; reviled; scorned; violated. *"Be quiet you bumbling idiot," profaned the cruel ruler, "and listen to what I have to tell you."*

Professed: affirmed, claimed or declared openly. Affirmed one's belief in. Claimed skill or knowledge of. Admitted; announced; confirmed; contended; maintained; purported. *"I believe that our candidate is the most qualified to be elected the next president of the union," the campaign spokesperson professed.*

Proffered: offered freely and unselfishly for acceptance or rejection. Extended; proposed; suggested; volunteered. *"Perhaps this small donation will benefit your cause," proffered the rich man.*

Prohibited: forbade by authority or law. Curbed; denied; disallowed; hampered; hindered; precluded; prevented. *"You are not allowed to smoke anywhere in the residence halls," prohibited the director of campus housing.*

Projected: directed one's voice so as to be heard clearly from a distance. Conveyed one's ideas, feelings, etc. to others effectively. Attributed something such as an emotion to someone other than oneself. Described; outlined; proposed; transmitted. *"Can everyone in the back hear me?" projected the speaker.*

Promised: committed oneself by a declaration assuring that one will or will not do something; made an oath. Guaranteed; pledged; vouched; vowed. *"From this day forward, I will serve you well and honorably, with my very life if need be," the knight promised as he knelt before the king.*

Promoted: contributed to the establishment, growth or progress of. Urged the adoption of. Advanced; advocated; cultivated; enhanced; furthered; supported. *"This combination of herbs and vitamins will not only provide you with the minimum daily requirement of essential vitamins and minerals, it will give you more energy to perform your daily tasks," promoted the sales rep.*

Prompted: moved or inspired by suggestion. Assisted by providing the next words; jogged the memory. Cued; incited; motivated; prodded; pushed; reminded; spurred. *"That is the question," prompted the Shakespearean coach.*

Pronounced: uttered in a clear, correct or accepted manner. Stated or declared officially or formally. Articulated; decreed; enunciated; judged; proclaimed; vocalized. *"From this day forth, September eighteenth will be a day to remember" pronounced the monarch.*

Prophesied: predicted or revealed the future as if by divine guidance. Forecast; foretold; forewarned; portended; warned. *"There will be a great famine in our land," the seer prophesied.*

Proposed: put forth for acceptance, consideration or discussion. Recommended another for a membership, office or position. Introduced; nominated; presented; submitted; suggested. *"I believe this new gimmick will put our little company on the map," proposed the chairperson. "What do the rest of you think?"*

Proscribed: denounced or forbade the practice, use, etc. of. Banished; condemned; disapproved; outlawed; prohibited; repudiated. *"Pets will no longer be allowed in this apartment building," the owner proscribed.*

Protested: made a formal declaration of disapproval or spoke strongly against. Avowed; boycotted; contended; disagreed; disputed; dissented; objected; renunciated. *"Higher wages and better benefits or we won't work," protested the female employees.*

Proved: established the authenticity, truth or validity of through argument or evidence. Affirmed; certified; corroborated; demonstrated; substantiated; supported; upheld; verified. *"All the tests show that this toothpaste does indeed whiten and brighten your teeth better than any of the other leading brands," proved the manufacturer.*

Provided: made available. Made a condition or set down as a stipulation. Afforded; arranged; bestowed; conferred; furnished; rendered; supplied. *"Each of you have been given a map and compass," provided the platoon sergeant. "Now it's up to you to find your way back to camp without being captured by the enemy before nightfall."*

Provoked: excited to some action or feeling. Angered; annoyed; inflamed; irritated; maddened; roused; stirred up. *"You're lousy at this game! You'd all be better suited for sandlot baseball than the majors," provoked the coach.*

Publicized: drew public attention to. Acclaimed; advertised; announced; broadcast; heralded; promoted. *"The war is over! The war is over!" publicized the young man selling newspapers on the street corner.*

Puffed: breathed forcefully and rapidly. Filled or swelled with conceit or pride. Exaggerated; exhaled; flattered; gasped; heaved; panted; wheezed. *"I can't . . . go any further," the marathon runner puffed exhaustedly.*

Pumped: obtained information by questioning another closely or persistently. Cross-examined; grilled; interrogated; probed. *"So, you are telling me that you know absolutely nothing about this crime?" pumped the attorney.*

Punctuated: emphasized or stressed through periodic interruption. Inserted stops. *"I already told you, I DON'T FEEL LIKE GOING OUT TONIGHT," punctuated the irate woman.*

Purported: professed, claimed or gave the often false appearance of being or intending. Alleged; declared; implied; objected. *"You didn't have to wash the dishes, mom, I was going to do that later,"* the *teenager purported.*

Purred: made or uttered a low vibratory sound such as that of a contented cat. *"Oh, Douglas, say that to me again,"* purred the young *lady in love.*

Pushed: urged on vigorously or persistently. Encouraged; incited; inspired; motivated; persuaded; pressured; prodded; prompted; propelled; spurred. *"That's it, Leroy, keep going, you can do it,"* *pushed the coach.*

Puzzled: pondered a problem, question or riddle in an effort to solve or understand it. Brooded; mulled; perplexed; wondered. *"How can there be videotaped evidence of him being at the scene of the crime, when a room full of people swear that he was at a party that very same night?"* puzzled the detective.

-Q q-

Quaked: shuddered or trembled as from cold or some strong emotion such as fear. Quavered; quivered; shivered; shook. *"Please don't eat me, Mr. Ogre,"* the little girl quaked.

Qualified: described by enumerating the characteristics or qualities of. Declared or made legally competent or capable. Made less harsh or severe. Authorized; empowered; enabled; licensed; moderated; modified; sanctioned. *"Let's see, you have straight A's, didn't miss any classes in the past year and were active in several school organizations. You should have no problem getting accepted into this university,"* qualified the dean.

Quarreled: engaged in an angry dispute. Found fault with. Argued; bickered; complained; differed; disagreed; disputed; squabbled. *"I can't believe you had the nerve to go on vacation without telling me, and on top of that, I had to find out from Lana that you were gone," quarreled the fiancee.*

Quavered: spoke in a tremulous or quivering voice. Quivered as from weakness. Quaked; shook; shuddered; trembled; trilled; vibrated. *"What–what are you going to do with me?" quavered the young woman fearfully.*

Quelled: crushed, subdued or put a forcible end to. Allayed; calmed; pacified; quenched; quieted; squelched; suppressed. *"People, return peacefully to your homes or we will be forced to take serious measures," quelled the national guard.*

Queried: expressed doubt or uncertainty about. Put a question to or called into question. Asked; disputed; distrusted; inquired of; quizzed; searched. *"Are you quite certain about those test results?" the surgeon queried.*

Questioned: expressed uncertainty about. Sought a reply to an inquiry. Asked; challenged; disputed; distrusted; doubted; interrogated; queried. *"I don't quite buy your story, Alexander. Are you certain you are not forgetting to tell me something?" questioned mother suspiciously.*

Quibbled: evaded the main point by emphasizing a petty detail. Found fault with or criticized for petty reasons. Argued; bickered; carped; dodged; hassled; nit-picked. *"Dinner was great, Karen, it's just that you know I can't stand eating off of plastic plates," Chuck quibbled.*

Quieted: calmed or pacified; brought to rest. Allayed; comforted; hushed; silenced; stifled; stilled. *"It's okay, honey," quieted the young mother, "the storm is over and you can go back to sleep now."*

Quipped: made a clever, witty, often sarcastic remark. Bantered; gibed; jested; put-down. *"I went out on a blind date last night. My friend told me the young woman had a pop bottle figure, but he didn't add that it was a two liter bottle," the comic quipped .*

Quivered: shook with a slight, rapid, tremulous movement. Quaked; shivered; shuddered; twitched; trembled. *"I--I'm sorry, granny, I didn't mean to break the music box," quivered Marissa nervously.*

Quizzed: questioned closely or repeatedly, or to test the knowledge of. Asked; examined; interrogated; queried; tested. *"All right class, question number one. Who was the first president of the United States?" quizzed the third grade teacher.*

Quoted: repeated or copied a brief passage or excerpt from, or the words of another with acknowledgment of the source. Cited; recalled; reproduced; retold. *"Ask not what your country can do for you, ask what you can do for your country," the historian quoted .*

-R r-

Raged: spoke or acted in a furiously intense or violent manner. Boiled; exploded; fumed; rampaged; ranted; seethed; stormed. *"Get out! Get out of this house you lazy, good-for-nothing bum," raged the father.*

Railed: uttered criticisms or objections in abusive, bitter or harsh language. Carried on; declaimed; fulminated; ranted; raved; scolded. *"What sort of incompetent moron are you?" railed the customer. "Not only did you burn the food, you brought me the wrong order!"*

Raised: put forward for consideration. Caused to come about. Uttered or voiced. Advanced; aroused; awakened; inspired; instigated;

provoked; stirred up. *"I would like to see a new computer system put in the library," raised Mrs.Quincy at the PTA meeting.*

Rallied: summoned or called together for a common purpose; brought to action. Recovered abruptly from a disadvantage or setback. Teased good-humoredly or mocked playfully. Assembled; bantered; collected; convalesced; gathered; revived; ridiculed. *"C'mon team, I know they beat us once before but let's get out there and kick some butt," rallied the coach. "I know you can do it!"*

Rambled: spoke or wrote aimlessly without connecting ideas. Drifted; meandered; wandered. *"Car . . . black car . . . ran over the dog . . . hit the man on the lawn . . . cut grass . . . smelled just like watermelon . . . dead," the disturbed man rambled.*

Ranted: expressed in a loud, extravagant or violent fashion. Bellowed; blustered; harangued; raved; spouted; stormed. *"You haven't seen the last of me," the retreating commander ranted, "I'll be back!"*

Rasped: uttered in a harsh, grating tone. *"Water!" the dying man rasped, "I need water."*

Rated: calculated the value of or placed in a particular rank or grade. Expressed disapproval or found fault with. Appraised; assessed; berated; estimated; rebuked; scolded. *"Your car is in great condition and should sell for more than book value," rated the appraiser.*

Ratified: approved or gave official sanction to. Affirmed; authorized; certified; confirmed; endorsed; validated. *"July fourth shall henceforth be known as Independence Day," ratified the politicians.*

Rationalized: devised superficially logical or plausible explanations or excuses for one's actions, beliefs, words, etc. Accounted for; justified; made allowances for. *"I started smoking because it's cool and everyone else does it," the teenager rationalized.*

Rattled: uttered a quick succession of sharp, short sounds. Spoke rapidly or effortlessly. Blathered; chattered; gabbed; prattled. *"Black bug's blood," rattled Devon repeatedly.*

Raved: spoke wildly, irrationally or incoherently. Uttered with great enthusiasm or in a frenzied fashion. Roared or raged at. Babbled; bubbled; effervesced; fumed; gushed; ranted; stormed. *"Wow, look at that hot air balloon!" raved the young boy. "I want to ride in one someday!"*

Read: spoke aloud written or printed material. Foretold or predicted the future. Determined the intent or mood of, or attributed a certain interpretation or meaning to. Delivered; discerned; perceived; recited; translated. *"Florence, you seem to be a little down today," read the counselor. "Would you like to talk about it?"*

Reasoned: argued or talked logically and persuasively. Figured; rationalized; thought through. *"If you work hard now and get good grades you'll be able to afford your dream car and much more one day," reasoned the guidance counselor.*

Reassured: assured again or restored confidence in. Bolstered; cheered; comforted; encouraged; inspired. *"This story will be a best seller someday very soon," the editor reassured the new author.*

Rebelled: felt or expressed repugnance or strong unwillingness; defied, resisted or refused allegiance to an authority or accepted convention. Deserted; dissented; insurrected; mutinied; revolted. *"I will not fight merely for the sake of fighting," rebelled the knight. "I will lift my sword only if the cause is just."*

Rebuffed: refused bluntly and often disdainfully. Ignored; repelled; repulsed; slighted; snubbed. *"Your ideas for this ad campaign are totally unusable," rebuffed Mr. Zane. "If you plan on being a part of this team you had better come up with something workable by 9:00 a.m. tomorrow."*

Rebuked: blamed, criticized or scolded in a sharp manner. Admonished; berated; censured; chided; reproved; reprimanded. *"Shame on you, Albert," his mother rebuked, "you broke grandma's favorite vase."*

Rebutted: refuted, especially by providing opposing arguments or evidence. Contradicted; denied; disagreed; repelled; retorted. *"The eyewitness claims to have seen my client at the scene of the crime, but I can prove beyond a shadow of a doubt that the witness is lying," rebutted the defense attorney.*

Recalled: brought back to awareness or to mind. Recollected; remembered. *"When I was a child," grandma recalled, "things were much different than they are today."*

Recanted: withdrew or renounced formerly held beliefs or statements in a formal or public manner. Disavowed; disclaimed; repudiated; rescinded; retracted; revoked. *"It seems that our previous report regarding the demise of Senator Lloyd in a plane crash was incorrect," recanted the anchorman.*

Recapped/Recapitulated: repeated briefly in concise form. Recounted; reiterated; restated; summarized. *"Once again, the final score in the state championship was Lincoln seventeen, Washington fourteen," the sportscaster recapped.*

Reciprocated: made some sort of return for something done or given. Acted likewise; alternated; interchanged; returned the compliment. *"Thanks for all your help, Ava. Let me take you out to a nice dinner tomorrow evening as a small token of my appreciation," reciprocated her aunt.*

Recited: said aloud or repeated something memorized or rehearsed before an audience. Delivered; narrated; performed; quoted; said by heart. *"Twinkle, twinkle little star, how I wonder what you are," the first grader recited.*

Reckoned: counted on or considered as being. Assumed; calculated; computed; deemed; figured; judged; regarded as; thought. *"Three yards of material ought to be enough to make that pretty dress you want," reckoned the seamstress.*

Recognized: acknowledged and/or accepted the authority, existence, genuineness or validity of. Acknowledged as worthy of appreciation or approval. Admitted; discerned; identified; knew; understood. *"Today we will give a special award to the young men and women of the police force who went above and beyond the call of duty," recognized the mayor.*

Recoiled: shrank back as in fear. Cowered; cringed; demurred; flinched; winced. *"I can't go any further, Sarge," recoiled the soldier. "I–I don't want to die!"*

Recollected: recalled to mind with some effort. Placed; remembered. *"Let's see now, it was 1929 when the Great Depression began," the old man recollected.*

Recommended: commended or suggested favorably as being worthy or desirable for some position or use. Advised or counseled. Advocated; encouraged; endorsed; favored; prescribed; proposed. *"Take these pills twice a day for fourteen days and you should be feeling fine in no time at all," recommended the doctor.*

Reconciled: brought into harmony or made friendly again. Adjusted; corrected; restored; settled. *"Daddy's real sorry for missing your school play, honey. Tell me what can I do to make it up to you," reconciled father.*

Recounted: gave an account or narrated the facts or particulars of. Detailed; related; told. *"My date was wonderful, first we went to a fine restaurant where we had chicken marsala, then to the theatre to see the latest off-Broadway play," Ashley recounted happily to her friend*

Recriminated: replied to an accuser with a countercharge; accused in return. *"I can prove where I was the night the store was robbed. Can you?" recriminated the accused thief.*

Rectified: put or set right. Adjusted; amended; corrected; fixed; remedied. *"It was me, mom," Timothy rectified. "I'm the one who accidentally broke the television set."*

Redeemed: compensated or made up for. Restored the honor, reputation or worth of. Reclaimed; recouped; recovered; reformed; regained. *"Your actions have more than compensated for your crimes. I give you back your family and title," redeemed the ruler.*

Reeled: felt dizzy or giddy; lurched, staggered or swayed as in drunkenness. Rocked; spun; tottered; weaved; wobbled. *"I believe I have had enough to drink," reeled Les as he headed for the door. "Good night, gentlemen."*

Referred: directed to a source for help or information. Directed the attention of or made a reference or allusion to. Alluded; cited; consulted; mentioned; submitted. *"You can get counseling through any of the agencies on this list," referred the doctor.*

Reflected: formed or expressed carefully considered thoughts about; thought seriously about. Deliberated; meditated; pondered; speculated. *"My life would have been much different had I married Edmond for love, and not for his money and title," Lois reflected sadly.*

Refused: declined to accept, agree to, allow, consider, do or grant. Denied; disallowed; forbade; prohibited. *"Absolutely not," Vanessa refused adamantly. "I will not lie just to protect your sorry butt."*

Refuted: proved to be false or erroneous; denied the accuracy or validity of. Challenged; contradicted; invalidated; rebutted. *"Sir, your theories regarding the origins of life are preposterous," refuted the philosopher. "They are the ravings of a madman at best."*

Regarded: gazed or looked at attentively; observed closely. Took into account or considered. Admired; appreciated; heeded; reflected; scrutinized; thought. *"There's something different about the way you look today,"* regarded Lewis. *"I know, you got your hair cut."*

Regretted: felt disappointed, distressed or sorry about, or mourned over someone or something. Bemoaned; bewailed; grieved; lamented; moaned. *"Gerald, my love, how could I have been so foolish as to let you go,"* regretted Rosalind tearfully.

Regulated: controlled, directed or governed according to a law, principle or rule. Put in or maintained order. Adjusted; guided; handled; managed; organized; supervised. *"From now on the no smoking ban will be strictly enforced in all government buildings,"* regulated the politician.

Rehashed: went over again in another form with significant alteration; discussed again. *"As I told Wayne and Stacy earlier, I am very disappointed with the cast's performance during yesterday's rehearsal,"* rehashed the drama coach.

Rehearsed: practiced or recited in preparation for a public or formal performance. Drilled; narrated; prepared; readied; repeated. *"Romans, countrymen, lend me your ears,"* the actor rehearsed.

Rejected: refused to take, agree to, accept, believe, consider or grant. Discarded or threw out as substandard, useless or worthless. Denied; disdained; dismissed; spurned. *"No, you're wrong!"* rejected Theresa vehemently. *"Trevor loves me, not Fiona."*

Rejoiced: was glad, happy or delighted; was full of joy. Celebrated; exulted; reveled. *"Children, come quickly, your father has returned home from the war,"* mother rejoiced as she ran to the door.

Related: narrated, recounted or told a story or gave an account of. Conveyed; described; disclosed; divulged; revealed. *"They managed to* *stay alive in the desert for five days without any food or water and only a limited amount of shelter," the doctor related in amazement.*

Relented: became more compassionate, forgiving or lenient. Softened in attitude or temperament. Bended; capitulated; gave way; yielded. *"Come here, child and have some dinner," grandmother relented, "you have been punished sufficiently for your ill conduct."*

Relinquished: regretfully let go of something or someone. Abandoned; abdicated; ceded; gave up; surrendered; waived; yielded. *"Though I fear letting you go, I know that I must," relinquished the young bride. "Hurry back to me, my love."*

Relished: took keen or zestful pleasure in. Appreciated; delighted; enjoyed; fancied; rejoiced in; savored. *"I just love it when you play the piano and sing to me," relished Jill. "Please don't stop."*

Remarked: expressed briefly or made a casual observation. Took notice of. Commented; mentioned; noted; regarded; surveyed. *"You look very handsome tonight," remarked the pleased wife.*

Remembered: brought an image or thought back to mind; awakened memories of. Recalled; recollected. *"I've had a few cats in my time, but Tiger was the friendliest and most playful of them all," Felisha remembered with a hint of sadness.*

Reminded: caused to remember; brought to mind. *"Don't forget that you have basketball practice tonight at seven," reminded mother.*

Remonstrated: said or pleaded in complaint, objection or protest. Argued; demonstrated; differed; disputed; dissented. *"I was not parked illegally," remonstrated the driver, "therefore, I don't feel that I should have to pay this fine."*

Rendered: gave, relinquished, submitted or surrendered what is due or owed. Delivered or pronounced formally. Accorded; construed;

granted; interpreted; presented; supplied; translated. *"Here is the money I owe you for the car," rendered Evan. "Do you think I can have the title now?"*

Reneged: failed to carry out a commitment or promise. Renounced or disowned. Backed out; repudiated; withdrew. *"Sorry, Rich, I know it's short notice but I can't be the best man at your wedding after all," reneged Vaughn apologetically. "Jeanie's dad is in the hospital and I feel like I should be there with her."*

Renounced: gave up something usually by formal public statement. Cast off or disowned. Abandoned; abdicated; disavowed; recanted; resigned; waived. *"As of January first, I will no longer be the head of the Salem police department," the Chief renounced sadly.*

Repealed: revoked or withdrew officially or formally. Annulled; canceled; invalidated; rescinded; terminated; voided. *"Dancing is no longer considered a crime," repealed the Council of Morality.*

Repeated: stated or did something again. Duplicated; echoed; mimicked; reiterated; replicated. *"I said, TURN THE RADIO DOWN!" father repeated loudly.*

Repelled: refused to accept, agree or submit to. Warded off or drove back. Deflected; foiled; opposed; resisted; withstood. *"Back! Back you evil sorcerer into the fiery pits of Hades from whence you arose," repelled the white knight with the sacred talisman.*

Repented: felt remorse or regret for what one has done or failed to do. Bemoaned; deplored; lamented; was contrite. *"Father, please forgive me for I have sinned," the young priest repented.*

Rephrased: stated again in a clearer or different way. *"Perhaps I wasn't clear the first time so I'll ask you again. Were you in any way involved in the murder of Justin Fletcher?" rephrased the patient attorney.*

Replied: answered or responded in speech or action. Acknowledged; came back with; countered; rejoined; retorted. *"That sounds good to me," replied Felix enthusiastically. "I'm so hungry I'll eat just about anything."*

Reported: carried back an account of or information about someone or something repeating it to another. Announced; communicated; disclosed; divulged; recounted; revealed. *"There are seven squadrons of fighter jets heading your way," reported the pilot.*

Reprehended: found fault with something done. Censured; criticized; rebuked; reproved. *"This building is not up to code," reprehended the safety inspector, "and cannot be opened to the public until each violation has been properly dealt with."*

Reprimanded: reproved severely especially in a formal or official way, or by a person in authority. Admonished; castigated; chided; lectured; reproached; scolded. *"You have disgraced yourself and this company, Mr. Brooks," reprimanded the CEO. "You're fired!"*

Reproached: expressed criticism or disapproval of, or disappointment in another. Admonished; blamed; condemned; rebuked; vilified. *"I can't believe that you were foolish enough to try drugs after all our talks about the physical and psychological dangers associated with their use," reproached mother.*

Reproved: found fault with or conveyed disapproval of. Admonished; chastened; rebuked; reproached; scolded. *"If you studied more and played video games less perhaps you would be passing algebra," reproved father.*

Repudiated: strongly rejected the authority or validity of; strongly rejected as false, unfounded or unjust. Abolished; canceled; disavowed; disowned; nullified; rescinded. *"Just because one little laboratory concluded that fluoride in water protects teeth from cavities doesn't mean that their results are infallible," repudiated the professor.*

Repulsed: rebuffed or rejected with coldness, denial, indifference or rudeness. Avoided; ignored; repelled; shunned; spurned. *"The sight of you makes me sick, Roger. I don't ever want to see you again," repulsed the young lady.*

Requested: expressed a wish or desire for. Asked; entreated; petitioned; solicited; sought. *"Waiter, could you bring another glass of water please?" requested the patron.*

Resented: felt or showed displeasure and hurt or indignation at or toward another from a sense of being injured or offended. *"So it's true. You do think I'm fat and unattractive," resented Abigail.*

Resisted: remained firm against or refused to cooperate with. Balked; combatted; contested; countered; opposed; withstood. *"My soldiers and I would rather die than surrender to the enemy of our king," resisted Sir Raymond.*

Resolved: made a firm decision about or found a solution to. Committed; decided; intended; proposed; solved. *"I think we should have the wedding at that little chapel on Third Street," resolved the groom-to-be.*

Resounded: sounded or uttered loudly. Celebrated or praised as in verse or song. *"Hail, King of Kings! Hail Lord of Lords," resounded the crowd.*

Responded: acted or replied in return or in answer. Acknowledged; recognized; rejoined. *"Yes, dear, whatever you say, dear," the bored husband responded.*

Rested: ceased voluntarily the introduction of evidence. Settled something such as an issue. Decided; determined; ended; halted; recessed; suspended. *"Ladies and gentlemen of the jury, you have heard the testimony and seen the evidence. All that remains is for you to bring in a verdict of not guilty," rested the attorney confidently.*

Restated: stated once more or anew. Repeated; rephrased. *"Once again, please remain seated until the car has come to a complete stop before exiting to your left,"* restated the ride attendant.

Resumed: began or went on after an interruption. Continued; proceeded; reembarked; reestablished. *"As I was saying,"* resumed the speaker as the crowd's applause died down, *"we need to stand firm, united in our cause, irregardless of personal loss or hardship."*

Retorted: made a verbal comeback in a caustic, quick or witty fashion turning the words of the previous speaker back upon that speaker. Answered; quipped; rebutted; replied. *"What do you know about exercise and diet? The only exercise you get is from stuffing your face with everything you see on your 'seefood' diet,"* retorted Rhonda.

Retracted: withdrew something or disavowed it. Abjured; abnegated; repealed; rescinded; took back. *"I know I said I would marry you, Blake, but I just can't,"* retracted his fiancee. *"I'm so sorry."*

Returned: reverted in thought or speech. Responded to. Answered; replied; retorted. *"Hmmm, yes, I suppose you're right,"* returned grandpa as he sucked thoughtfully on his pipe. *"This may well be the biggest catfish ever caught in these here parts."*

Revealed: made known something otherwise hidden or secret. Betrayed; disclosed; divulged; exposed; unearthed; unmasked; unveiled. *"Did you know that Walter and his wife have separated?"* the town gossip revealed.

Reveled: took great pleasure or delight in. Basked; celebrated; enjoyed; frolicked; relished; romped. *"I just love this amusement park,"* reveled Amber. *"I don't ever want to leave!"*

Revered: regarded with the deepest deference, devotion or respect. Awed; cherished; honored; worshipped. *"Nothing pleases me more than serving your majesty,"* revered the servant.

Reviled: used abusive or contemptuous language in speaking to or about. Assailed; berated; denounced; derided; scorned. *"Down on your worthless knees you spineless piece of dung,"* reviled the master.

Revised: reconsidered one's words and changed or modified them. Altered; corrected; doctored; emended; modified; revamped. *"You are correct, I did say that you would get a raise, BUT only if you land the McMaster account,"* revised the boss.

Revoked: annulled or voided by recalling, reversing or withdrawing. Canceled; disclaimed; invalidated; repealed; rescinded. *"The ban on fireworks in Jefferson Township has been lifted,"* revoked the trustee.

Reworded: expressed or stated again in other words; changed the wording of. Rephrased; restated. *"What I meant to say was, I would love to go to the dance with you on Friday night,"* reworded Amanda quickly.

Rhymed: composed poetry or verse which ends in a word that corresponds in sound to the last word of one or more other lines of the same poem or verse. *"Roses are red, violets are blue. I have a secret Valentine, can you guess who?"* the smitten girl rhymed happily.

Riddled: posed a question or statement requiring thought to answer, solve or understand. *"Why did the chicken cross the road?"* riddled Owen.

Ridiculed: spoke or acted in such a fashion so as to purposefully make another the object of scornful laughter by joking, mocking, etc. Derided; gibed; humiliated; insulted; jeered; joshed; taunted. *"That is the stupidest question I've ever heard,"* ridiculed the older sister.

Rivaled: attempted to equal or surpass. Battled with; clashed; competed with; contended with; outdid. *"I'm a much better athlete than you and today at the tryouts I'll prove it,"* rivaled the Olympic hopeful.

Roared: uttered a loud, deep rumbling sound as in distress, excitement, pain or rage. Talked or laughed loudly and boisterously. Bawled; bayed; bellowed; blustered; clamored; howled. *"DEFENSE! DEFENSE!" the home crowd roared.*

Romanced: thought, talked or behaved in a romantic manner. Allured; courted; flirted. *"Hey there, gorgeous, would you like to go out with me tonight?" romanced Patrick as he wrapped his arms about his wife's waist.*

Romanticized: had or upheld romantic attitudes, ideas, etc. *"Oh, if only he would just give me a chance, I know I could make him fall in love with me," romanticized Eileen.*

Romped: carried on or frolicked in a boisterous manner. *"Look mom, no hands," romped the little boy as he bounced wildly on his rocking horse.*

Rooted: gave audible encouragement or applause to a player or team. Lended moral support to someone. Acclaimed; backed; bolstered; boosted; cheered; hailed. *"Touchdown! Touchdown!" rooted the cheerleaders as the quarterback let the ball fly.*

Roused: stirred up or excited to anger or action. Aroused from apathy, depression or sleep. Animated; awakened; goaded; incited; provoked; spurred; summoned. *"Come on, Melvin, wake up or we'll be late for our plane," roused his best friend.*

Ruled: settled by decree; decided or declared authoritatively or judicially. Adjudged; concluded; determined; pronounced; resolved. *"All land west of the river to the edge of the mountains belongs to the people of Zanthos," King Octavius ruled.*

Rumbled: uttered with a deep long rolling sound. Boomed; resounded; reverberated; roared; thundered. *"Fe, fi, fo fum," the angry giant rumbled.*

Rushed: caused to move, act or speak with unusual haste or violence. Hurried; goaded; pressured; pushed; urged. *"Virgil, are you alright? Tell me what happened,"* rushed mother worriedly.

-S s-

Sacrificed: offered, gave or sold something valuable at less than its presumed worth. Forfeited; relinquished; renounced; surrendered. *"This table cost me $200 to make, but I'll sell it to you for half that amount,"* sacrificed the carpenter.

Saluted: acted, gestured or greeted with an expression of goodwill, respect, welcome or warm approval. Hailed; honored; nodded to; revered; waved to. *"Petty Officer Scott, reporting as requested,"* saluted the sailor.

Sampled: took a piece, portion or section of something in order to test or examine it. Analyzed; judged; partook of; tasted; tried. *"This chocolate is delicious,"* sampled Lindsay. *"Where did you get it?"*

Sanctified: gave moral, social or religious permission or approval thereby validating a course of action. Anointed; blessed; consecrated; legitimized; made holy; purified. *"I now pronounce you man and wife,"* sanctified the priest. *"You may kiss the bride."*

Sanctioned: gave official approval, authorization or permission. Allowed; assented; consented; endorsed; licensed; ratified; supported. *"All farmers may grow an additional crop of corn this year due to the overwhelming need for it,"* sanctioned the governor.

Sang: uttered words or sounds with musical inflection. Caroled; chanted; crooned; hummed; intoned; lilted. *"We wish you a Merry Christmas,"* sang the spirited carolers.

Sassed: talked back disrespectfully, impertinently or impudently. *"I'm NOT going to my room because I don't WANT to," sassed the young child.*

Savored: appreciated fully. Delighted in; enjoyed; liked; relished; took pleasure in. *"Oh, man, this whirlpool is just what I needed," the football player savored after a hard fought game.*

Scathed: criticized or denounced severely. Was harsh or caustic with. *"You impudent little fool! How dare you speak to the queen that way," scathed the chambermaid.*

Schemed: contrived a plan especially a secret or devious one. Contrived an impractical or unrealistic plan. Arranged; connived; conspired; devised; plotted. *"If we wait until after dark, no one will see us when we bomb the cars with rotten eggs," schemed the pranksters.*

Schooled: trained or disciplined. Educated; instructed; taught. *"Two times two is four, two times three is six, two times four is eight," schooled the teacher.*

Scoffed: showed or expressed mocking contempt, derision or scorn. Belittled; derided; ridiculed; sneered. *"You think you can do better than me?" the fighter scoffed. "Get your butt in this ring and we'll see, pal?"*

Scolded: found fault with angrily; rebuked or chided severely or harshly. Berated; castigated; criticized; reprimanded; reproved. *"This ceiling is a disaster and you have the nerve to call yourself a painter," scolded the shift supervisor. "Go back and do it again and do it right this time."*

Scorned: expressed contempt or disdain for a person or object considered despicable or unworthy. Despised; rebuffed; repulsed; mocked; ridiculed; scoffed at. *"He's the worst mayor this city has* *ever had," scorned the voter. "Taxes are high and unemployment is even higher."*

Scowled: affected, expressed or influenced with an angry or displeased look. Frowned; glared; glowered; grimaced. *"Francis, I'm afraid this essay of yours is totally unacceptable," the teacher scowled. "If you want anything higher than an 'F' you'll have to do it again."*

Screamed: uttered a loud, piercing, shrill sound as from fear or pain. Laughed loudly or hysterically. Bellowed; hollered; howled; roared; screeched; shrieked; yelled. *"Someone help me, I've been robbed!" screamed the old lady whose purse had just been stolen.*

Screeched: uttered in a high-pitched strident voice. Cried; howled; pealed; screamed; squealed; shrieked. *"HELP, HELP, I'm drowning!" screeched the swimmer as he struggled against the waves.*

Scrutinized: examined or observed with great care; inspected critically. Explored; perused; probed; regarded carefully; searched. *"This art work looks like an original," scrutinized the buyer, "but I will need to get it appraised in order to be sure."*

Seconded: encouraged, promoted or reinforced. Endorsed a motion or nomination as a preliminary requirement to discussion or vote. Advanced; advocated; aided; favored; supported; upheld. *"I agree that Fredrica is the best person for this position," seconded Kirsten.*

Seduced: persuaded or tempted to evil, wrongdoing or improper conduct. Allured; beguiled; captivated; charmed; enticed; lured. *"C'mon, baby, your husband will never know if you spend the night at my place," seduced the handsome young man.*

Seethed: became violently agitated or excited; became livid. Blustered; boiled; fumed; smoldered; stewed. *"You idiot, look what you've done!" seethed the outraged diner. "You spilled coffee all over my new suit!"*

Selected: chose or picked out from among others. Elected; fancied; opted; preferred; settled upon; singled out. *"I choose Larry, Tyler, Vince and Mickey to be on my soccer team,"* selected the captain.

Sermonized: preached, especially in a dogmatic moralizing fashion. Admonished; harangued; lectured; rebuked; reproved. *"All who take the Almighty's name in vain will burn in hell's fire for all eternity,"* sermonized the radical young man.

Settled: reached a decision. Agreed; determined; reconciled; rectified; resolved. *"All right, the steak house it is,"* settled mother. *"Now can everyone please get ready to leave."*

Shivered: shook as from fear or cold. Quaked; quivered; shuddered; trembled. *"My word, it is s-so cold in this house,"* shivered Bonnie. *"I hope they get the electricity back on s-soon."*

Shouted: called or cried out loudly as in a sudden outburst or uproar. Bellowed; clamored; hollered; howled; yelled. *"HEY, UMPIRE!"* the irate fan shouted, *"YOU STINK!"*

Shrieked: uttered a shrill, often frantic cry in laughter, pain or terror. Hooted; screeched; squawked; squealed; yelped. *"FIRE! FIRE!"* shrieked the neighbor as he ran toward the burning house. *"Someone call 9-1-1!"*

Shrilled: uttered a high-pitched, thin, piercing sound. Blared; clamored; piped. *"I'll get you my, pretty,"* the wicked witch shrilled, *"and your silly little cat, too!"*

Shrugged: raised the shoulders in a gesture of disdain, doubt or indifference. *"I don't care,"* Monica shrugged. *"You choose which hotel to stay in."*

Shuddered: shook or trembled suddenly and violently as from fear or revulsion. Convulsed; fluttered; jerked; quaked; quivered; shivered.

"Did–did you see that headless man?" shuddered the boy at the haunted house.

Shushed: demanded silence from another or others. Hushed; quieted; silenced. *"Enough,"* shushed the substitute teacher. *"You've heard the assignment, now get to work."*

Shied: felt uneasy in the presence of others or shrank from others due to a bashful or timid nature. Cowered; demurred; recoiled; was reticent; withdrew. *"It was really nice meeting you, but I–I really have to go now,"* shied Kristen.

Sighed: took in and let out with a long, deep audible breath as in fatigue, longing, relief, sorrow, etc. Breathed; brooded; grieved; groaned; lamented; moaned; yearned. *"Whew,"* Trey sighed as he wiped his sweaty brow. *"I sure am glad that I'm through giving that speech to the class."*

Signified: denoted or made known as with a sign or word/s. Bespoke; conveyed; evinced; expressed; implied; indicated; manifested. *"'Fourscore and seven years ago, our fathers brought forth on this continent a new nation,' are the words with which Lincoln began his famous speech at Gettysburg,"* signified the historian.

Silenced: made still or quiet; curtailed the expression of. Calmed; curbed; deadened; hushed; quelled; stifled; suppressed. *"Everyone,"* silenced the speaker, *"if you'll find a seat we can begin."*

Simmered: was filled with pent-up emotion or was in a state of gentle ferment. Boiled; chafed; fumed; seethed; stewed. *"I can't believe this has happened to me twice in the same day,"* Vincent simmered as he changed yet another flat tire on his old car.

Simpered: smiled or uttered in a silly, self-conscious, often coy fashion. Giggled; grinned; smirked; snickered; tittered. *"Gosh, do you really think that I'm pretty?"* Nina simpered to her prom date.

Sized: made an estimate, judgment or opinion of. Classified; graded; summed. *"This shade of blue should match the truck,"* sized the owner.

Skirted: avoided something controversial or difficult. Circumvented; detoured; evaded; shunned. *"I'm sorry, honey, I just don't have time to talk about this right now,"* skirted Greg. *"It'll have to keep."*

Slapped: criticized or insulted sharply in order to injure another's pride, self-respect, etc. Cut; rebuffed; rejected; snubbed. *"If I didn't know for a fact that you're my son I would never believe it,"* slapped the angry mother.

Slashed: verbally criticized or lashed another sharply. *"What makes you think the prince would allow such a pathetic, ugly thing as you at his ball?"* the evil stepmother slashed cruelly.

Slighted: treated as if of small importance or with discourteous reserve or inattention. Affronted; disdained; disregarded; insulted; overlooked; snubbed. *"You there, here's $10 to take those pieces of luggage to our room immediately,"* slighted the aging film star.

Slipped: made a slight error or oversight in conduct, speech, thinking or writing. Blundered; erred; goofed; made a mistake. *"Oh, blast it, I forgot to mail that letter again,"* slipped Glenda as she drove past the post office.

Slobbered: expressed enthusiasm or sentiment effusively or incoherently. Gushed; sputtered. *"Happy New Year! Another round for me and my friends,"* slobbered Darrell.

Slurred: pronounced indistinctly. Spoke disparagingly or slightingly of or treated without due consideration. Affronted; defamed; ignored; insulted; maligned; mumbled; muttered; sullied. *"Hey there, sexy, wanna dance with old Spence?"* slurred the inebriated man as he stumbled toward the pretty blonde.

Slurped: ate or drank noisily with a loud sipping or sucking sound. Lapped. *"This soup is great, mom," slurped Brad, "can I have some more?"*

Smeared: stained or attempted to destroy or harm the reputation of. Accused; libeled; maligned; slandered. *"Your current governor spends your tax dollars on wild parties and private jets," his opponent smeared. "Is that the sort of person you want running this state?"*

Smiled: expressed with an upward curving of the corners of the mouth and a sparkling of the eyes indicating amusement, derision or pleasure. Beamed; favored; grinned; smirked. *"It is such a pleasure to finally meet you, Mrs. Tyrus," smiled Samantha. "I've heard so many wonderful things about you."*

Smirked: smiled in a conceited, knowing or self-satisfied manner. Grimaced; grinned; simpered; sneered. *"When all is said and done we'll see who's holding the trophy," the hockey team captain smirked.*

Smoothed: made less harsh or crude, or made calm or tranquil. Allayed; assuaged; mollified; refined; soothed. *"There, there, child, it was just a nightmare," smoothed the old nanny.*

Snapped: spoke or uttered abruptly or sharply as in anger. Barked. *"Sit down and behave!" snapped the old lady at the rambunctious child.*

Snarled: growled angrily, threateningly or in a hostile manner. Barked; lashed out; snapped. *"So! You think that you can out conjure me, do you?" the wizard snarled, "Well I'll show you a thing or two."*

Sneered: spoke in a contemptuous, derisive or scornful fashion. Belittled; disdained; jeered; leered; mocked. *"I am Thor the Mighty," sneered the giant. "Who are you to challenge me, little man?"*

Snickered: uttered or laughed in a derisive or sly partly stifled manner. Cackled; giggled; simpered; sniggered; snorted. *"Look at that stupid clown on the stilts,"* snickered the child. *"He can hardly stand up on them."*

Sniffed: uttered in a contemptuous or haughty manner. Disdained; disparaged; mocked; scoffed. *"That's Vera Johnson,"* sniffed the wealthy widow, *"she lives on the OTHER side of town."*

Sniffled: wept or whimpered lightly. Blubbered; cried softly; whined. *"I lost my puppy and can't find him anywhere,"* sniffled the little boy as he wiped a tear from his eye.

Sniped: made malicious underhanded remarks or attacks. *"What a shameless young woman you are, stuffing your big bottom into those tight pants,"* sniped the old woman.

Sniveled: complained or fretted in a tearful, whining way. *"But I don't want to go to school today, mommy,"* sniveled Pat.

Snorted: made an abrupt noise expressive of anger, contempt, ridicule or scorn. Jeered; scoffed; sneered. *"You're such a fool, Parker,"* snorted Valerie. *"I only married you for your money."*

Snubbed: treated with contempt, disdain or scorn; behaved coldly toward. Ignored; rebuffed; repudiated; slighted. *"I have nothing to say to you, Chloe,"* snubbed her stepdaughter. *"You're not my mother and you never will be."*

Snuffled: talked or sang in a nasal tone as due to a cold or allergy. *"Mom, my nose is all stuffed up and I can't breathe very well,"* snuffled Dwight miserably.

Sobbed: wept aloud with convulsive gasping breaths. Blubbered; cried; howled; wailed. *"He left me, dad, he left me at the alter,"* Ashley sobbed.

Softened: made less critical, harsh or strident. Lessened; mitigated; mollified; tempered. *"Honey, I'm sorry I yelled at you," softened Antonio, "I really didn't mean to."*

Solicited: asked or sought earnestly or by entreaty or persuasion. Tempted or enticed to do something evil, illegal or immoral. Appealed for; importuned; incited; pleaded; requested. *"Would you like to make a donation to the homeless shelter down the street? It is tax deductible, you know," solicited the volunteer.*

Solved: found or provided a satisfactory answer or explanation to; found a solution to. Deciphered; resolved; unraveled; untangled. *"Gosh, no wonder the stereo isn't working. It isn't plugged in," solved Brock.*

Soothed: calmed or eased as by gentle words or treatment. Alleviated; appeased; comforted; placated; relieved. *"Everything will be fine, Jenny," the baby-sitter soothed, "your mommy and daddy will be home soon."*

Sorted: arranged according to class, size, type, etc. Catalogued; classified; divided; grouped; specified. *"These old coupons need to be thrown out and replaced with new ones," sorted Arlene as she prepared the grocery list.*

Sounded: uttered distinctly. Made known or celebrated; expressed one's views vigorously. Announced; articulated; broadcast; declared; enunciated; pronounced; voiced. *"The war is over!" sounded the newscaster excitedly. "The communist party surrendered early this morning."*

Spared: treated with leniency or mercy, or refrained from treating harshly. Acquitted; held back; pardoned; protected; reprieved; saved. *"You have proven yourself to be a useful servant, Barnabas, so I will allow you to live," spared the ruler, "but the others who betrayed me will be hung at dawn."*

Sparred: bandied words about. Argued; disputed; wrangled. *"So you think you're such a lady-killer, do you, well let's just see who gets a date first," sparred the frat brother.*

Sparked: issued an enthusiastic response. Roused or spurred to action. Aroused; excited; incited; inspired; instigated; stimulated. *"We're the number one team in the American League so let's get out there and show that lame excuse for a team what we can do," sparked the head coach.*

Spat: expressed animosity or contempt suddenly and forcefully or with a hissing or sputtering noise. *"You make me SICK!" Cheryl spat. "How could you DO such a thing?"*

Specified: defined, described, mentioned or stated explicitly or in detail. Adduced; cited; denoted; designated; indicated; stipulated. *"Your next assignment is to make a navy blue skirt and a white blouse with lace around the collar and cuffs," the home economics instructor specified.*

Speculated: engaged in a course of reasoning often based on inconclusive evidence. Brooded; cogitated; conjectured; contemplated; deliberated; hypothesized; theorized. *"My bones are aching somethin' fierce. Must mean there's gonna be a storm soon," speculated the old farmer.*

Spilled: allowed or caused, especially accidentally or unintentionally. Let something secret be known. Blabbed; disclosed; divulged; revealed; told. *"Oh, I color Farrah's hair all the time. She's got a lot of grey for her age," spilled the beautician.*

Spluttered: spoke hurriedly or incoherently as when angry, confused, embarrassed or excited. Blustered; gibbered; hemmed and hawed; jabbered; mumbled; stammered; stumbled. *"Omigosh, did you just see that car run the red light and almost hit that lady?" Armand spluttered.*

Spoke: expressed emotions, ideas, opinions or thoughts orally. Articulated; commented; conversed; conveyed; expounded; talked; vocalized. *"Truth is knowledge that is innocent of error,"* spoke the wise old guru quietly.

Spooked: annoyed, frightened, made nervous or startled with words or actions. Alarmed; disturbed; intimidated; scared; terrified; terrorized. *"I'm going to chop off your head and eat you for dinner,"* spooked the ghoul at the haunted house.

Spouted: spoke or uttered in a loud, pompous manner, or in a rapid, ready flow of words. Blustered; carried on; harangued; gushed; pontificated; ranted; vented. *"Yesterday I bowled an eight hundred series,"* spouted Cliff. *"Let's see ya beat that!"*

Spurned: refused, rejected or treated with contempt or disdain. Cast aside; dismissed; mocked; repelled; repulsed; slighted; snubbed. *"I have no use for you any longer,"* spurned Queen Oletta. *"Leave me now!"*

Sputtered: spit out words or sounds in an excited or confused manner. Jabbered; mumbled; sprayed; stammered; stumbled. *"Wow! Did you see that home run?"* Collin sputtered as he leapt to his feet.

Squabbled: engaged in a disagreeable argument over a trivial matter. Battled; bickered; clashed; differed; quarreled; scrapped; wrangled. *"You did not win cause you cheated,"* squabbled the eldest twin.

Squawked: uttered a loud harsh cry or complained or protested especially in a loud or raucous voice. Blared; croaked; griped; grumbled; screeched; squalled. *"Give me back my doll!"* Hannah squawked.

Squeaked: emitted in a short thin shrill voice. Cheeped; chirped; screeched; shrieked; squealed; yelped. *"If you help me escape I'll grant you one wish,"* squeaked the tiny leprechaun.

Squealed: uttered or made a long shrill cry or sound. Bawled; cried; screamed; screeched; wailed; whined; yelled. *"Oh, that guitar player in the band is soooo cute," squealed the lovestruck teen.*

Squelched: put down or silenced as with a crushing retort. Hushed; quieted; squashed; suppressed; trampled. *"Be still, you pathetic fool!" squelched the mad scientist.*

Stalled: acted or spoke evasively or hesitantly so as to deceive or delay. Arrested; blocked; checked; impeded; interrupted; obstructed; postponed. *"Can you wait just a few more minutes?" stalled the passenger. "I'm sure my friend will be here soon."*

Stammered: said or spoke with involuntary blocks or pauses often with rapid repetitions of certain sounds or syllables. Faltered; fumbled; mumbled; spluttered; sputtered; stuttered. *"Would-would-would you like to g-go out with m–me?" stammered the bashful boy.*

Stated: set forth in words especially in a definite, formal or specific way. Declared; elucidated; expounded; narrated; presented; related. *"In order to graduate this year, every student must pass a scholastic competency exam," the principal stated emphatically.*

Stereotyped: expressed a fixed or conventional conception or notion of a group, idea or person. Categorized; pigeonholed; typecast. *"He's so tall and divinely handsome he must be an actor," stereotyped Susan.*

Stewed: fretted, fumed, or worried; was troubled or vexed. Boiled; chafed; fussed; grumbled; seethed; simmered. *"If this here drought continues I don't know if we'll be able to harvest enough crops to make it through the winter," stewed the plantation owner.*

Stifled: interrupted or cut off. Kept in or held back. Curbed; gagged; inhibited; muffled; repressed; restrained; smothered. *"Stop right there, young lady," stifled father. "I'm tired of your lame excuses."*

Stilled: made quiet, still or tranquil. Allayed; calmed; hushed; pacified; silenced; suppressed. *"There, there, Sondra, the prince will find a way to rescue us," stilled her brother.*

Stipulated: made an express condition, demand or provision in an agreement. Allowed; cited; designated; granted; guaranteed; indicated; pledged; warranted. *"I'll pitch the tent if you cook dinner," stipulated the camper.*

Stressed: placed emphasis, importance or significance on. Accented; affirmed; asserted; featured; underlined; underscored. *"When speaking Spanish you must roll the letter 'R,'" the language teacher stressed.*

Struggled: was strenuously engaged in a problem, task or undertaking. Battled; contested with; endeavored; exerted; labored; strained. *"No matter how many times I work it out, I just can't seem to get this algebra problem right," struggled the high school student.*

Studied: examined closely or gave careful thought to. Contemplated; deliberated; investigated; pondered; reflected; scrutinized. *"These cancer cells are fascinating," studied the pathologist.*

Stumbled: acted, proceeded or spoke in a clumsy, faltering or unsteady fashion. Blundered; bungled; floundered; made mistakes. *"What I meant to say, um, I-I mean what I was trying to say was, oh, never mind," Sylvester stumbled.*

Stuttered: spoke with a spasmodic repetition or prolongation of sounds. Faltered; fumbled; mumbled; spluttered; sputtered; stammered. *"Wha-wha-what did y-you a-a-ask me?" Malcolm stuttered nervously when the teacher called his name.*

Submitted: gave in to or subjected oneself to the authority, desires, power or will of another. Acceded; capitulated; complied; succumbed; surrendered; yielded. *"As you wish, master," submitted Igor as he sent bolts of electricity coursing through the creature.*

Substantiated: supported with evidence or proof. Authenticated; confirmed; corroborated; demonstrated; proved; verified. *"Colonel Mayo's fingerprints were found on the scissors which killed Mrs. Osterman proving that he is indeed the murderer," substantiated the detective.*

Succumbed: submitted to an overpowering desire or force; gave up or gave in. Acceded; capitulated; complied with; deferred to; surrendered; yielded. *"I can't take it anymore. I have to have a cigarette," succumbed the air traffic controller.*

Suggested: mentioned as something to consider or think over. Advocated; hinted; implied; insinuated; intimated; proposed; recommended. *"If the brand you're buying now isn't relieving your pain, perhaps you should try a different analgesic," the neurologist suggested helpfully.*

Sulked: was sullenly aloof or withdrawn as in silent resentment or protest. Brooded; grumped; moped; scowled; was disgruntled. *"I never get to play. All I ever do is sit on the bench," the reserve player sulked.*

Summed: reviewed or summarized briefly and in a condensed form. Abridged; capsulized; compressed; epitomized; outlined; summarized. *"Here's our itinerary for tonight's meeting. First we'll review last week's minutes, followed by the financial statement and end with current issues and ideas," summed the chairperson.*

Summarized: reviewed or summed briefly and in a condensed form. Abridged; capsulized; compressed; epitomized; outlined; summed. *"Romeo and Juliet is a story of two teens from rival families who fall in love only to die tragically," summarized the drama teacher.*

Summoned: requested to appear or called together. Convened; gathered; invoked; mustered; sent for; subpoenaed. *"Send for the court jester," summoned King Cyrus. "I wish to be entertained."*

Supplicated: asked or petitioned for earnestly or humbly. Appealed; begged; beseeched; entreated; implored; requested. *"Please, if you have any news of my daughter's whereabouts, please contact the police immediately," supplicated the kidnapped child's father.*

Supposed: regarded as genuine, true, etc. without actual knowledge or conclusive evidence. Assumed; conjectured; imagined; presumed; reckoned; surmised; suspected. *"This artifact may well be several thousand years old," supposed the archeologist.*

Surmised: imagined or inferred without sufficient evidence. Believed; concluded; deemed; guessed; hypothesized; supposed; theorized. *"The universe was formed when millions of atoms collided creating the cosmos as we know it today," the astronomer surmised.*

Surrendered: gave up, or resigned oneself to an emotion or the control of another. Abandoned; capitulated; conceded; relinquished; submitted; yielded. *"Hold your fire, I'm unarmed," surrendered the bank robber.*

Surveyed: examined comprehensively or inspected carefully. Analyzed; canvassed; observed; investigated; scrutinized. *"After reviewing the blueprints there seems to be a structural defect in the building's parking deck," surveyed the architect.*

Sustained: affirmed the truth or validity of. Confirmed; corroborated; maintained; proved; upheld. *"According to the most recent studies, aspirin is shown to reduce the risk of death from heart attacks," sustained the medical specialist.*

Swaggered: walked, expressed or conducted oneself insolently or arrogantly. Boasted; bragged; browbeat; bullied; paraded; strutted. *"I am the greatest dragon slayer in all the world," Ulysses swaggered.*

Swelled: was or became filled with indignation, pride, self-importance, etc. Was filled with emotion. Puffed up. *"I graduated cum laude from Princeton University," swelled Jacob.*

124

Swore: stated or affirmed earnestly and with great conviction. Made a solemn promise. Used obscene or profane language. Adjured; attested; blasphemed; cursed; pledged; vowed. *"I vow to serve you well, my Lord, even if it means my life," swore the faithful knight.*

Sympathized: expressed or felt compassion for another's plight or suffering. Shared or understood the ideas, opinions, thoughts, etc. of another. Accorded; agreed; commiserated; empathized; pitied. *"My condolences for your loss, Mrs. Hermann," sympathized the priest. "If I can be of any asistance you need only call."*

-T t-

Tattled: revealed the activities, plans or secrets of another. Blabbed; blathered; chattered; divulged; gossiped; snitched. *"Momma, momma, Sidney's got cigarettes in his room," tattled Debbie.*

Taunted: reproached in a contemptuous, insulting or mocking tirade. Derided; harassed; jeered; ridiculed; teased; tormented. *"You're so fat you can't even fit into your prom dress," the younger sister taunted.*

Teased: urged persistently. Annoyed, made fun of, or pestered playfully. Baited; coaxed; gibed; heckled; mocked; vexed. *"Can't you run any faster than that, shortie?" teased the older children during recess.*

Tempted: enticed, induced or persuaded to do wrong especially by a promise of reward. Allured; aroused; bewitched; charmed; seduced; tantalized. *"If you steal the Tiger's Eye and bring it to me, I will grant you life eternal," tempted Tatianna.*

Terrorized: overpowered another by instilling intense fear. Coerced another into doing or saying something through intimidation or fear.

Alarmed; dismayed; frightened; horrified. *"If you dare try to escape my dungeon my three-headed serpent will eat you alive,"* terrorized Xerxes.

Testified: made a declaration of fact or truth under oath. Affirmed; attested; bore witness; submitted testimony. *"Yes, sir, that's him in the grey suit. He's the one I saw breaking into the store that night,"* the witness testified.

Thanked: expressed appreciation or gratitude. Held responsible for. Acknowledged; blamed; blessed; credited; was grateful. *"Oh, what a thoughtful gift!"* thanked the delighted newlyweds. *"We appreciate your generosity."*

Theorized: formulated an assumption based on limited information or knowledge. Conjecture; hypothesized; imagined; presumed; speculated. *"The sun is the center of our universe, not the earth,"* Copernicus theorized.

Thirsted: had a strong, insistent craving or desire. Coveted; lusted; relished; yearned. *"I just can't get enough of this book,"* thirsted Winona as she eagerly turned the page.

Thought: determined, resolved or worked out by pondering, reasoning or reflection. Believed; deliberated; devised; imagined; speculated; supposed; visualized. *"A pizza sure sounds good for dinner,"* Jessie thought hungrily.

Threatened: expressed an intention to inflict evil, injury, pain or punishment. Forewarned; intimidated; menaced; terrorized; warned. *"Give up the jacket or die, punk,"* threatened the gang leader.

Thundered: expressed loud vociferous remarks or threats angrily, commandingly or violently. Boomed; exploded; pealed; resounded; roared; rumbled. *"Get that rusty old bucket moving!"* thundered the irate driver.

Thwarted: defeated, frustrated, hindered or opposed another's ambitions, efforts, plans, etc. Barred; checked; foiled; inhibited; obstructed; prevented; staved off. *"Caught you with your hand in the cookie jar again," thwarted Cathy. "You know you have to eat dinner before you can have treats."*

Timed: expressed or recorded the speed or duration of. *"Good job, Reggie, you ran the mile in four minutes, fifty-three seconds," timed the coach.*

Tittered: laughed in a half-suppressed way suggesting nervousness or silliness. Chuckled; giggled; smirked; snickered; teeheed. *"Look! He's actually coming over here," tittered the awkward teen.*

Toasted: spoke prior to raising a glass and drinking in the honor of someone or something. Celebrated; commemorated; complimented; saluted. *"May your days be filled with sunshine, laughter and love," the best man toasted.*

Told: gave a detailed account or narrative of. Gave instructions to. Informed positively. Assured; chronicled; communicated; directed; depicted; made known; notified; revealed. *"Once upon a time in a land far, far away there lived a beautiful princess," told Maximillion.*

Tolerated: allowed or put up with without opposing or prohibiting. Bore; consented to; endured; indulged; permitted; sanctioned. *"Now, Sandie, you know I'm not real fond of that type of music, but I'll let you listen to it if you keep it turned down," tolerated aunt Stella.*

Tormented: caused great physical pain or mental anguish. Agitated; annoyed; harassed; irritated; persecuted; pestered; troubled. *"I'll call you every night until you agree to go out with me," tormented Darren.*

Tortured: brought great physical pain or mental anguish upon another. Extorted information by subjecting to mental or physical pain or suffering. Abused; distressed; maltreated; mistreated; tormented. *"Hang the prisoner by his heels until he agrees to talk,"* tortured the commandant.

Totaled: determined the amount of. Added; calculated; computed; figured; summed. *"That'll be one hundred sixty-two dollars and ninety-five cents,"* totaled the cashier.

Touted: praised, promoted or recommended highly or energetically. Acclaimed; celebrated; exalted; extolled; glorified; vaunted. *"This luxury vehicle has such a smooth ride, you'll think you're gliding on ice,"* touted the car dealer.

Toyed: amused oneself idly. Treated casually or without seriousness. Dallied; played with; trifled. *"You certainly are a strong, handsome young man,"* toyed the barmaid. *"Can I get you anything special?"*

Trailed: subsided or became gradually fainter. Diminished; dwindled; grew weak; lessened; tapered off. *"My comrades will free me, you'll see . . ."* the prisoner trailed as he was dragged off by the storm troopers.

Translated: expressed in another language. Put into different words or simpler terms. Clarified; deciphered; elucidated; explained; interpreted; paraphrased; reworded. *"Joie de vivre means hearty or carefree enjoyment of life,"* translated the French teacher.

Transmitted: passed information along. Caused to go or sent from one person or place to another. Broadcast; communicated; conveyed; dispatched; passed on; relayed. *"Bravo one niner, you are clear to land,"* transmitted the tower to the circling aircraft.

Treasured: kept or regarded as highly valuable or precious. Cared greatly for. Appreciated; cherished; held dear; prized; revered; valued. *"This gold locket is so beautiful. I'll never take it off,"* treasured Mona.

Trembled: shook involuntarily as from anger, anxiety, excitement, fear or weakness. Felt anxiety or fear. Fluttered; quaked; quivered; panicked; pulsated; shivered; shuddered. *Please, don't hurt me," the teller trembled as the desperate young man waved his gun at her.*

Tricked: cheated or deceived through a mischievous or playful act or illusion. Bluffed; duped; misled; outfoxed; outwitted; swindled; victimized. *"Gotcha!" tricked Nicole as her friend spit out the bitter tasting candy.*

Trifled: acted, performed or spoke jokingly as with little seriousness or purpose. Jested; played with; toyed; treated lightly. *"Oh, this old thing? I've had it forever," trifled Shelly.*

Trilled: sang or uttered with a fluttering or tremulous sound. Quavered; warbled. *"Oh, what a lovely day!" the gardener trilled.*

Triumphed: exulted or rejoiced over a success or victory. Overcame; prevailed; vanquished; won. *"Xavier has killed the mighty dragon!" triumphed the townspeople.*

Trolled: sang gaily or heartily. *"We wish you a merry Christmas, and a happy New Year," the carolers trolled.*

Trumpeted: uttered or proclaimed loudly. Gave forth a resounding call. *"Hear ye, hear ye," the town crier trumpeted, "the king wishes to invite one and all to a great feast this very eve."*

Trusted: had or placed confidence in. Placed in the care of another. Assured; believed; confided; depended on; entrusted; hoped; relied. *"Sure, I'll let you borrow my car because I know you're a cautious driver," trusted Melinda.*

Tutored: gave individual instruction to. Coached; drilled; mentored; taught. *"Before you even turn on the car you should fasten your seat belt and adjust your rearview mirror," tutored the driving instructor.*

Twaddled: talked or wrote in a foolish or senseless manner. Babbled; chattered; driveled; prattled. *"This little piggy went to market and this little piggy huffed and puffed and blew gramma's house down," twaddled the young child to her stuffed toys.*

Twittered: uttered or trembled with nervous agitation or excitement. Spoke in a rapid, tremulous manner expressive of agitation, timidity, etc. Giggled nervously. Chattered; fluttered; giggled; tittered; warbled. *"Omigosh, Denise, you will never guess in a million years who I saw at the mall today!" twittered Pamela.*

-U u-

Uncovered: made known, disclosed or revealed. Divulged; exposed; manifested; unearthed; unveiled. *"Dr. Courtney, come quick, I think I've found the secret entrance to the tomb of Ahkmanon," uncovered her assistant.*

Underacted: understated intentionally. Underplayed. *"That flu shot wasn't so bad," underacted the older sister. "Now it's your turn, Maggie."*

Underplayed: dealt with, expressed or presented subtly or with restraint. Underacted. *"I've seen much worse," underplayed the officer as she surveyed the wreckage. "The important thing is that everyone walked away unharmed."*

Underscored: stated with emphasis. Drew attention to. Accentuated; heightened; intensified; stressed. *"You go to your room RIGHT NOW, young lady," underscored mother, "and I do mean RIGHT NOW!"*

Understated: expressed or stated less completely or truthfully than seems warranted by the facts, or, with restraint or lack of emphasis, especially with irony. *"That new ride the Mind Scrambler isn't any big deal,"* understated Norman, *"IF you don't mind scrambled eggs for brains."*

Understood: had comprehension or knowledge of, or sympathy or tolerance for. Accepted; appreciated; empathized; recognized; was aware of. *"I know how you feel right now, Paula, I lost my mother a few years ago from the same illness,"* understood her best friend.

Undertook: committed, pledged or took upon oneself. Attempted; began; commenced; endeavored; shouldered; tackled. *"I volunteer to help with set design,"* undertook the theatre student. *"I've never had the chance to work behind the scenes before."*

Unearthed: brought to light or made known. Brought to the public's attention. Discovered; displayed; dug up; divulged; exhibited; revealed; uncovered. *"These, ladies and gentlemen, are the most recent artifacts excavated from the burial grounds of the Nambundi tribe in South America,"* unearthed the archeologist on the exhibit's opening day.

Unfolded: revealed gradually by written or spoken explanation. Disclosed; divulged; explained; explicated; recounted. *"Stephanie was at the party the night of the murder, but she was also observed leaving the murder scene. She could be in two places at once because,"* unfolded the detective, *"Stephanie has an identical twin."*

Unified: combined or made into one. Allied; consolidated; fused; incorporated; merged; wed. *"Today the kingdoms east and west of the river Seleria will come under one rule,"* unified the king.

United: brought together in common cause, interest, opinion, etc. Allied; blended; coupled; joined; merged; pooled; wed. *"The feud between Amazons and Centaurs is no more. From this day forward we will live in peace and harmony, for the greater good of all,"* united Queen Hippolytes to the cheers of her tribe.

Unloaded: expressed or told freely something which burdens or troubles. Disclosed; divulged; poured forth; unburdened; vented. *"Dad, I'm responsible for Toby spraining his arm," unloaded Nate apologetically. "We were goofing around on the playground and I sort of got carried away."*

Upbraided: rebuked bitterly or severely. Gave a tongue-lashing to. Admonished; berated; castigated; censured; denounced; reprimanded; reproached. *"Dominic, how could you be involved in such a cruel and thoughtless prank? Your father and I raised you better than that!" upbraided mother.*

Updated: brought up to date on the most recent facts, ideas or methods. Overhauled; renovated; revised; upgraded. *"For those of you unable to make last month's meeting, we began to discuss plans for the upcoming Halloween ball," updated the secretary.*

Upheld: maintained or affirmed against opposition. Gave moral or spiritual encouragement or support to. Acknowledged; advocated; approved; championed; defended; sustained. *"I swear, Mrs. Dexter, I did not cheat on the test," Maureen upheld.*

Uplifted: raised to a higher emotional, intellectual, moral, social or spiritual level or condition. Advanced; bettered; elevated; enriched; improved; refined. *"You are a wonderful, caring, beautiful young woman. Everyone there will love you, honey," uplifted the shy girl's mother.*

Upped: raised or bet more than another or others. Increased; inflated; made higher. *"I'll see your bet and raise you fifty more," upped the gambler.*

Upstaged: drew attention or praise to oneself at the expense of another. Treated haughtily. *"Don't forget, were it not for my generous donations, this silly little play would have faded into obscurity long ago," upstaged the benefactress.*

Urged: forced or drove forward or onward. Entreated earnestly and often repeatedly. Appealed; beseeched; exhorted; goaded; impelled; prodded. *"Come on, Troy, you can do it, you can finish the race," the marathon runner's family urged.*

Usurped: seized another's authority, possessions, etc. by force and without legal right. Appropriated; commandeered; infringed upon; stole; took for oneself. *"You're old and unable to rule with any real authority, so I am taking over as king of Utopia," usurped the ailing man's nephew.*

Utilized: put to use; made practical or profitable use of. Capitalized on; employed; resorted to. *"All the material for my artwork came from dumpsters and junkyards," utilized the aspiring young artist proudly.*

Uttered: expressed, produced or spoke audibly. Articulated; declared; enunciated; exclaimed; proclaimed; pronounced; voiced. *"Wow, will you look at this!" uttered Leo excitedly. "I just found a sack full of crisp one hundred dollar bills!"*

-V v-

Validated: declared or made legally valid. Established the soundness of. Authenticated; certified; corroborated; enacted; ratified; sanctioned. *"Here's the deed to your brand new house," validated the title clerk, "she's all yours, folks."*

Valued: determined or estimated the desirability, value or worth of. Regarded highly. Appraised; appreciated; assessed; cherished; held in high esteem; respected; treasured. *"Francesca, I'm so glad you're my friend," valued Paige. "Thanks for being there when I really needed you."*

Vaunted: uttered extravagant self-praise. Boasted; bragged; flaunted; gloated; swaggered. *"So, you dare to challenge the greatest archer in all the land," Apollo vaunted. "I hope you enjoy losing."*

Venerated: regarded or worshipped with respect, reverence or heartfelt deference. Admired; adored; extolled; glorified; honored; idolized. *"I just love his work. He is by far the most talented sculptor of his time," venerated the art student.*

Vented: gave often forceful expression or utterance to strong pent-up emotions or thoughts. Aired; expressed; voiced; uttered. *"You are making me absolutely crazy! I am going out for a drive," vented Thelma.*

Ventilated: discussed or examined in public; brought out into the open. Broadcast; circulated; criticized; dissented; reviewed; spread. *"I feel it's time the issue of same sex marriage was finally addressed in a serious manner," the activist ventilated.*

Ventured: exposed to, or proceeded despite possible danger or risk. Expressed at the risk of censure, criticism or denial. Attempted; chanced; dared; endeavored; gambled. *"I don't care if the tide is coming in, I'm swimming over to that little island to see what's on it," ventured Clark.*

Verbalized: expressed oneself in words. Expressed oneself using an excessive number of words. Said; spoke; uttered; voiced; was wordy. *"Santa, I've been such a good little boy this year. I haven't kicked the dog or pulled my sister's hair and I even ate all my vegetables, so I should get everything I want for Christmas this year," verbalized Jeremy.*

Verified: proved to be true by demonstration, evidence or testimony. Authenticated; certified; documented; established; substantiated; validated. *"Yes, sir, it is true that smokers have a higher risk of heart disease than nonsmokers," the cardiologist verified.*

Vexed: annoyed in a petty, nagging fashion. Brought distress or suffering to. Afflicted; badgered; bothered; irritated; pestered; plagued; tormented. *"Anthony you are constantly late getting home from work while dinner sits on the table getting cold,"* vexed his wife. *"Why can't you be on time just once in your life?"*

Viewed: thought of in a particular way. Considered; contemplated; judged; perceived; regarded. *"I think we have no business being there and should withdraw all our troops immediately,"* viewed the cabinet member.

Vindicated: cleared of accusation, blame, doubt or suspicion with supporting arguments or proof. Defended, maintained or insisted on the recognition of one's rights. Absolved; acquitted; advocated; excused; exonerated; justified. *"The real murderer has confessed to the crime. You are free to go, Mr. Matthews,"* vindicated Judge Washington.

Violated: desecrated or profaned something sacred. Blasphemed; defiled; dishonored; transgressed; was sacrilegious. *"Yeah, I broke into that church and stole that golden cup they use,"* violated the punk. *"What of it?"*

Visualized: formed a mental image of something. Daydreamed; envisioned; fancied; imagined; pictured. *"I can see myself lying on a warm sandy beach, the sun beating down on my oiled skin, a cool drink nestled in my hand,"* Melanie visualized.

Vituperated: rebuked or criticized harshly or abusively. Berated; blamed; censured; found fault with; scolded; tongue-lashed. *"You idiotic moron, you! How could you do such a stupid thing?"* Victoria vituperated.

Vocalized: gave utterance to. Aired; articulated; expressed; spoke; uttered; vented; verbalized. *"La, la, la, la, la, la, la,"* the singer vocalized in preparation for her performance.

Vociferated: uttered something or cried out loudly and vehemently especially in protest. Demanded to be heard. Clamored; shouted; was outspoken. *"Save the whales, save the whales," vociferated the angry mob.*

Voiced: gave utterance to. Aired; articulated; disclosed; divulged; expressed; revealed; said; spoke; uttered; vented; verbalized. *"I think that it is high time we had a little discussion," Dean voiced assertively.*

Voided: made invalid. Abolished; annulled; canceled; countermanded; recanted; repealed; repudiated; rescinded; revoked. *"The ban on alcohol at frat parties has been lifted," voided the director of student activities.*

Volunteered: offered to do charitable or helpful work or performed a service without pay and of one's own free will. Extended; proffered. *"I'll go to the grocery store for you, Mrs. Conner," the neighbor graciously volunteered.*

Voted: expressed a choice, opinion or preference for, often by casting a vote. Chose; decided; declared; elected; selected. *"I'm in favor of the scary movie," Perry voted enthusiastically.*

Vouched: gave personal assurances or a guarantee. Substantiated by supplying evidence. Affirmed; attested to; backed up; certified; confirmed; endorsed; maintained; upheld. *"Mary is one of our most reliable and conscientious employees," vouched Mr. Bailey.*

Vowed: made a solemn pledge, promise or threat to do, get, etc. Affirmed; asserted; assured; resolved; swore; vouched. *"You haven't seen the last of me. I'll be back," the villain vowed as he made his escape.*

136

-W w-

Waffled: spoke or wrote in a wordy, vague or indecisive manner. Was evasive. *"Gee, I don't know, fast food sounds good, but then again, so does a nice steak dinner,"* Belinda waffled.

Wagered: risked or staked something on an uncertain outcome. Assumed; bet; gambled; hazarded; speculated; surmised; ventured. *"Let's see, put five dollars on Bonnie Blue in the third and five on Rags to Riches in the fourth,"* wagered Drew.

Wailed: emitted a long, loud high-pitched cry as of grief, pain or protest. Bawled; bemoaned; caterwauled; groaned; lamented; moaned. *"Ow! My knee!"* Mark wailed as he cradled the injured leg.

Waived: gave up or relinquished. Put aside or put off until later. Deferred; disclaimed; postponed; renounced; shelved; surrendered. *"No, I don't need an attorney before I answer your questions,"* waived Shirley.

Warbled: sang with trills or other melodic embellishments. Quavered; trilled; vibrated. *"Tra, la, la, twiddely de de,"* Chrissy warbled happily as she swept the floor.

Warmed: became affectionate, friendly, kindly or sympathetic to. Became animated, ardent, enthusiastic or spirited. *"Oh, you brought me some beautiful flowers. Come let momma give you a big hug,"* warmed Kathryn.

Warned: made aware of potential danger, evil or harm in advance. Admonished another's actions, speech, etc. Advised; alerted; cautioned; counseled; forewarned; informed; notified. *"The enemy is coming. I can see them marching over yon hill,"* warned Tobias.

Warranted: guaranteed or attested to the accuracy, character, condition, quality or reliability of. Granted authorization or sanction to do something. Affirmed; avowed; certified; empowered; licensed; permitted; swore. *"This particular brand of stereo will give you endless hours of listening pleasure," warranted the sales person.*

Waved: signaled or expressed with an up-and-down or back-and-forth movement of the hand or some other object. Gesticulated; gestured; motioned. *"Yoohoo, Aunt Gladys," waved her niece, "over here!"*

Wavered: expressed doubt or indecision; found it hard or was unable to decide. Trembled or quavered in sound, as of the voice. Faltered; fluctuated; hesitated; vacillated. *"Dad, I just can't decide whether to go to law school or medical school," wavered Donald.*

Weighed: considered the pros and cons of in order to make a choice or decision. Deliberated; evaluated; investigated; pondered; reflected; researched. *"A sports car is fun to drive but not very practical, whereas a mid-sized sedan is practical AND luxurious," weighed Veronica. "I guess I'll get the sedan."*

Welcomed: entertained, greeted or received another or others cordially or hospitably. *"Well, if it isn't Rebecca Vernon! My God, it's good to see you again," welcomed her old friend at their twenty year class reunion.*

Wept: expressed emotion such as anguish, grief or sorrow by shedding tears. Bawled; cried; lamented; mourned; sobbed; whimpered. *"Mommy, mommy, my blankie is missing," wept Rickie sadly.*

Wheedled: obtained, persuaded or attempted to persuade through the use of flattery or guile. Beguiled; cajoled; charmed; coaxed; enticed; induced; lured. *"Honey, you look so handsome tonight it would be a shame not to show you off at dinner and a movie," Brooke wheedled.*

Wheezed: uttered with a hoarse, whistling breathy sound. Gasped; hissed; huffed; panted; puffed. *"My God, this cold is going to kill me," wheezed Victor miserably.*

Whimpered: made low intermittent whiny sounds. Blubbered; complained; cried; sniffled; sniveled; sobbed. *"No one asked me out to the school dance Friday night," Callie whimpered.*

Whined: uttered a plaintive, high-pitched, somewhat nasal sound as in complaint, distress or fear. Begged or complained in a childish fashion. Fretted; griped; grumbled; moaned; sniveled; whimpered. *"But mom, I don't wanna go to school today," whined Craig pitifully. "Can't I stay home?"*

Whispered: spoke quietly or softly often saying or telling something that is private or secret. Gossiped; hinted; murmured; muttered; rumored; uttered under the breath. *"Be very quiet when we cross the bridge," Iggy whispered. "We don't want to wake up the trolls."*

Whooped: uttered a loud shout or cry of enthusiasm, exultation or excitement. Cheered; hooted; hollered; howled; hurrahed; roared; yelled. *"Yeeeeehaaaaaaw!" the rodeo cowboy whooped as he rode the bucking bronco.*

Willed: made a choice. Yearned for. Induced, tried to induce or resolved by sheer force of will. Chose; decided; decreed; desired; determined; dictated; ordered; wished. *"I refuse to allow you to frighten me," willed the brave hostage.*

Winced: shrank or started involuntarily, usually with a grimace as in alarm, distress, embarrassment or pain. Cowered; cringed; drew back; flinched; recoiled. *"Don't beat me, master!" winced the hunchback. "I wish only to serve your greatness."*

Winked: signaled or expressed by closing and opening the eyelid of one eye quickly and deliberately. *"Hey, there, big boy," Ivanna winked, " why don't you come up to my room for a nightcap."*

Wished: had or expressed a desire, longing or strong inclination for someone or something. Aspired; craved; hoped; hungered; pined;

thirsted; yearned. *"A nice red, juicy apple sure would be great right about now," the hungry little boy wished.*

Withheld: refrained from disclosing, giving, granting or permitting. Held back; kept secret; reserved; suppressed. *"Name, rank and serial number is all you'll get from me and nothing else," withheld the POW.*

Withstood: endured, opposed or resisted successfully. Bore; braved; defied; suffered; tolerated; weathered. *"I'll stay up all night studying if I have to in order to ace this test," withstood Dustin.*

Witnessed: took note of, was present at or had personal knowledge of. Furnished or served as evidence. Attested to; observed; noticed; testified; verified. *"The man in the blue sedan ran the red light, lost control of his car and careened through the grocery store's plate glass window," one of the other motorists witnessed.*

Wondered: had a feeling of admiration, awe, curiosity, doubt or surprise. Was amazed, dazed, dumbstruck, flabbergasted or stunned. Marvelled; pondered. *"Do you think we'll ever really know if there is intelligent life on other planets?" wondered Elizabeth.*

Wooed: sought the affections of another with romantic intentions. Courted; entreated; importuned; invited; pursued; solicited; tempted. *"I brought you some candy and your favorite flowers," wooed Kenneth. "I hope you like them."*

Worried: felt anxious, distressed, troubled or uneasy. Agonized; brooded over; cared; dreaded; fretted; stewed over; was dismayed. *"Gosh, I hope my old car can make this trip," worried Roz.*

Worshipped: regarded with adoring or ardent esteem or devotion. Admired; adulated; exalted; glorified; idolized; praised; revered. *"Great god, Osyrus, your servants kneel humbly before you," worshipped the high priestess.*

Wreaked: expressed anger, malice, rage, resentment, etc. Brought about; caused; inflicted; retaliated; vented. *"I'm gonna toss you out onto the street if you go on my carpet one more time!" wreaked the angry pet owner.*

Writhed: suffered great emotional distress as from embarrassment, revulsion or pain. *"God! I hope the rescue team finds me soon," the injured mountain climber writhed.*

-Y y-

Yakked/Yacked: talked persistently or meaninglessly. Babbled; chattered; prattled. *"And do you know that my little Townsend is so bright that he can actually read his storybooks and before you know it, he'll be balancing my checkbook," the proud mother yakked.*

Yammered: complained peevishly or whimperingly. Talked loudly and volubly. Bellowed; clamored; griped; grumbled; shouted; whined. *"Awww, do I have to eat all my vegetables before I can have dessert?" yammered Gretta.*

Yapped: talked noisily or stupidly. Blathered; chattered; gossiped; jabbered; prattled; tattled. *"Yeah, and up your nose with a rubber hose," the little leaguer yapped.*

Yawned: uttered wearily while or as if while yawning as a result of boredom, drowsiness or fatigue. *"The party was terrific, Carole," yawned Edwin, "but I have to be at work early tomorrow so I guess I'll say good night."*

Yawped: talked coarsely, loudly or raucously. Uttered a sharp cry. *"Hey, you little brats!" the old man yawped. "Get those bikes off my grass!"*

Yearned: felt sympathy or tenderness, or had a strong melancholy desire. Ached; craved; languished; longed for; pined; pitied. *"I sure wish I was back home eating mom's homemade apple pie right now,"* yearned the college student.

Yelled: expressed or uttered with a loud cry or shout as in enthusiasm, fright, pain or surprise. Cheered; clamored; hooted; squealed; whooped; yelped. *"V-I-C-T-O-R-Y is the Panther's battle cry,"* the cheerleaders yelled over the roar of the crowd.

Yelped: cried out sharply as in pain. Cried shrilly; screamed; shrieked; squealed; yelled. *"Oh, GOD! Someone call 9-1-1,"* the bystander yelped. *"I've been shot!"*

Yielded: gave up as in defeat. Gave way to argument, influence, entreaty, force or persuasion. Acceded; bowed; capitulated; caved in; deferred; succumbed; submitted; surrendered. *"As you wish, Sire,"* yielded the captain of the guard, *"I shall release the prisoners immediately."*

Yowled: uttered a long mournful cry. Bayed; caterwauled; screeched; wailed. *"Please,"* yowled the distraught woman, *"please don't leave me in this horrible place all alone."*

-Z z-

Zinged: criticized sharply or attacked verbally. *"Hanging out with you is about as exciting as watching paint dry,"* zinged Renee.

Quick Reference Guide

A
Abjured
Acceded
Accepted
Acclaimed
Accused
Acknowledged
Acquiesced
Added
Addressed
Adhered
Adjured
Admired
Admitted
Admonished
Advised
Advocated
Affirmed
Agreed
Alerted
Alleged
Allowed
Alluded
Amended
Announced
Answered
Appealed
Applauded
Approved
Argued
Articulated
Ascertained
Ascribed
Asked
Aspired
Assailed
Assented
Asserted
Assessed
Assuaged
Assumed
Assured
Atoned
Attacked
Attempted
Attested
Authorized
Averred
Avouched
Avowed

B
Babbled
Bade
Badgered
Baited
Balked
Bandied
Bantered
Bargained
Barked
Bawled
Bayed
Beamed
Beckoned
Begged
Began
Belched
Belittled
Bellowed
Bemoaned
Berated
Blabbered
Blackmailed
Blamed
Blanched
Blared
Blasphemed
Blasted
Blazed
Blessed
Blinked
Blistered
Blubbered
Bluffed
Blundered
Blurted
Blushed
Blustered
Boasted
Boiled
Booed
Boomed
Bossed
Bowed
Bragged
Brayed
Breathed
Bribed
Bridled

Quick Reference Guide

Bristled
Brooded
Bubbled
Bullied
Burped
Burst
Bustled
Buzzed

C
Cackled
Cajoled
Calculated
Called
Canted
Capitulated
Carped
Castigated
Caterwauled
Caviled
Celebrated
Censured
Certified
Challenged·
Championed
Chanted
Charged
Chastised
Chatted
Chattered
Checked
Cheered

Chided
Chimed
Choked
Chortled
Chuckled
Cited
Clacked
Claimed
Clamored
Clapped
Clarified
Clowned
Coached
Coaxed
Coddled
Coerced
Comforted
Commanded
Commandeered
Commemorated
Commenced
Commended
Commented
Commissioned
Communed
Communicated
Compared
Compelled
Competed
Complained
Complimented
Complied
Compromised
Computed

Conceded
Concluded
Concurred
Condemned
Condescended
Conferred
Confessed
Confided
Confirmed
Confronted
Congratulated
Conjectured
Conjured
Connived
Consented
Considered
Consoled
Conspired
Contemplated
Contended
Continued
Contradicted
Contributed
Contrived
Conversed
Conveyed
Cooed
Corrected
Corroborated
Coughed
Counseled
Countered
Courted
Craved

Quick Reference Guide

Cried
Cringed
Criticized
Croaked
Crooned
Cross-examined
Crowed
Cued
Cursed

D
Damned
Dared
Debated
Decided
Declaimed
Declared
Declined
Decreed
Decried
Deduced
Deemed
Defamed
Defended
Deferred
Defied
Delighted
Demanded
Demurred
Denied
Denigrated
Denounced

Depicted
Deplored
Deprecated
Derided
Described
Designated
Desired
Despaired
Despised
Determined
Diagnosed
Dictated
Differed
Digressed
Directed
Disagreed
Disallowed
Disapproved
Disavowed
Disbelieved
Disclaimed
Disclosed
Discounted
Discriminated
Discussed
Disdained
Dismissed
Disobeyed
Disparaged
Dispatched
Disproved
Disputed
Disregarded
Dissented

Dissuaded
Distracted
Diverged
Diverted
Divined
Divulged
Documented
Dodged
Dominated
Doted
Doubted
Drafted
Drawled
Dreaded
Dreamt
Drilled
Driveled
Droned
Drooled
Dubbed

E
Eased
Echoed
Editorialized
Effervesced
Elaborated
Elbowed
Elucidated
Embellished
Emphasized
Empowered

Quick Reference Guide

Enchanted
Encouraged
Endured
Enforced
Enjoined
Ensured
Entertained
Enthused
Enticed
Entranced
Entreated
Enumerated
Enunciated
Envied
Espoused
Established
Estimated
Eulogized
Evaded
Evaluated
Evoked
Exacted
Exaggerated
Exalted
Examined
Exclaimed
Excused
Exhaled
Exhorted
Exorcised
Expanded
Explained
Exploded
Exploited

Exposed
Expounded
Expressed
Extolled
Extorted
Extracted
Exulted
Eyed

F
Fabricated
Faked
Falsified
Faltered
Fancied
Faulted
Fawned
Feared
Feigned
Feinted
Fidgeted
Fielded
Figured
Finessed
Finished
Fired
Fished
Flagged
Flailed
Flared
Flattered
Flaunted

Flinched
Flirted
Flouted
Flushed
Fluttered
Forbade
Foretold
Forgave
Forswore
Framed
Fretted
Froze
Frolicked
Frowned
Fumed
Fussed

G
Gabbed
Gagged
Gambled
Gaped
Gasped
Gauged
Gawked
Gazed
Gestured
Gibbered
Giggled
Glanced
Glared
Gloated

Quick Reference Guide

Glowed
Glowered
Goaded
Gossiped
Granted
Greeted
Grieved
Grilled
Grimaced
Grinned
Griped
Groaned
Groped
Groveled
Growled
Grumbled
Grunted
Guaranteed
Guessed
Guffawed
Guided
Gulped
Gurgled
Gushed

H
Haggled
Hailed
Harangued
Harassed
Harped
Heaved

Heckled
Hedged
Held
Helped
Hemmed
Heralded
Hesitated
Hiccupped
Hinted
Hissed
Hollered
Hooted
Hounded
Howled
Huffed
Humphed
Hushed
Hustled

I
Identified
Illuminated
Illustrated
Imagined
Imitated
Imparted
Implicated
Implied
Implored
Imposed
Improvised
Impugned

Incited
Incriminated
Indicated
Indicted
Inferred
Informed
Inhaled
Inquired
Insinuated
Insisted
Inspired
Instigated
Instructed
Insulted
Interceded
Interjected
Interpreted
Interrogated
Interrupted
Intervened
Intimated
Intoned
Introduced
Invited
Invoked
Iterated

J
Jabbered
Jeered
Jested
Joined

Quick Reference Guide

Joked

Joshed

Jostled

Judged

Justified

K

Keened

Kidded

L

Labeled

Labored

Lamented

Lampooned

Languished

Lashed

Lauded

Laughed

Launched

Lavished

Leaked

Lectured

Led

Leered

Lessened

Leveled

Levied

Liberated

Licensed

Lied

Likened

Lilted

Limited

Lingered

Liquidated

Lisped

Listed

Loathed

Lobbied

Longed

Lurched

Lured

Lusted

Luxuriated

M

Maintained

Maligned

Managed

Mandated

Maneuvered

Manipulated

Manufactured

Mapped

Marveled

Masqueraded

Masterminded

Meddled

Mediated

Meditated

Menaced

Mentioned

Mesmerized

Mimicked

Minced

Minimized

Mistrusted

Moaned

Mocked

Mollified

Monkeyed

Moped

Moralized

Motioned

Motivated

Mourned

Mouthed

Mumbled

Munched

Murmured

Mused

Muttered

N

Nagged

Named

Narrated

Needled

Negated

Negotiated

Nibbled

Nodded

Nominated

Quick Reference Guide

Noted
Notified
Nudged

O

Obeyed
Objected
Observed
Obsessed
Obtested
Obtruded
Offered
Ogled
Opined
Opposed
Opted
Orated
Ordained
Ordered
Organized
Owned

P

Paced
Pacified
Painted
Paled
Paltered
Pampered
Panicked

Panted
Paraded
Paralleled
Paraphrased
Pardoned
Parlayed
Parleyed
Parroted
Parried
Patronized
Pattered
Paused
Pecked
Peeped
Penalized
Peppered
Performed
Perjured
Perked
Permitted
Persecuted
Persevered
Persisted
Persuaded
Pestered
Petitioned
Philosophized
Picked
Pictured
Pieced
Pinched
Pined
Piped
Piqued

Pitied
Placated
Plagued
Planned
Pleaded
Pledged
Plied
Plodded
Plotted
Pointed
Poked
Policed
Polled
Pondered
Pontificated
Posed
Postulated
Pouted
Practiced
Praised
Prattled
Prayed
Preached
Predicted
Preened
Preferred
Prescribed
Presented
Pressed
Pressured
Presumed
Pretended
Prevailed
Primed

Quick Reference Guide

Primped
Prioritized
Proceeded
Proclaimed
Prodded
Produced
Profaned
Professed
Proffered
Prohibited
Projected
Promised
Promoted
Prompted
Pronounced
Prophesied
Proposed
Proscribed
Protested
Proved
Provided
Provoked
Publicized
Puffed
Pumped
Punctuated
Purported
Purred
Pushed
Puzzled

Q

Quaked
Qualified
Quarreled
Quavered
Quelled
Queried
Questioned
Quibbled
Quieted
Quipped
Quivered
Quizzed
Quoted

R

Raged
Railed
Raised
Rallied
Rambled
Ranted
Rasped
Rated
Ratified
Rationalized
Rattled
Raved
Read
Reasoned
Reassured
Rebelled
Rebuffed

Rebuked
Rebutted
Recalled
Recanted
Recapped
Reciprocated
Recited
Reckoned
Recognized
Recoiled
Recollected
Recommended
Reconciled
Recounted
Recriminated
Rectified
Redeemed
Reeled
Referred
Reflected
Refused
Refuted
Regarded
Regretted
Regulated
Rehashed
Rehearsed
Rejected
Rejoiced
Related
Relented
Relinquished
Relished
Remarked

Quick Reference Guide

Remembered
Reminded
Remonstrated
Rendered
Reneged
Renounced
Repealed
Repeated
Repelled
Repented
Rephrased
Replied
Reported
Reprehended
Reprimanded
Reproached
Reproved
Repudiated
Repulsed
Requested
Resented
Resisted
Resolved
Resounded
Responded
Rested
Restated
Resumed
Retorted
Retracted
Returned
Revealed
Reveled
Revered

Reviled
Revised
Revoked
Reworded
Rhymed
Riddled
Ridiculed
Rivaled
Roared
Romanced
Romanticized
Romped
Rooted
Roused
Ruled
Rumbled
Rushed

S

Sacrificed
Saluted
Sampled
Sanctified
Sanctioned
Sang
Sassed
Savored
Scathed
Schemed
Schooled
Scoffed
Scolded

Scorned
Scowled
Screamed
Screeched
Scrutinized
Seconded
Seduced
Seethed
Selected
Sermonized
Settled
Shivered
Shouted
Shrieked
Shrilled
Shrugged
Shuddered
Shushed
Shied
Sighed
Signified
Silenced
Simmered
Simpered
Sized
Skirted
Slapped
Slashed
Slighted
Slipped
Slobbered
Slurred
Slurped
Smeared

Quick Reference Guide

Smiled	Squabbled	Swore
Smirked	Squawked	Sympathized
Smoothed	Squeaked	
Snapped	Squealed	
Snarled	Squelched	
Sneered	Stalled	**T**
Snickered	Stammered	Tattled
Sniffed	Stated	Taunted
Sniffled	Stereotyped	Teased
Sniped	Stewed	Tempted
Sniveled	Stifled	Terrorized
Snorted	Stilled	Testified
Snubbed	Stipulated	Thanked
Snuffled	Stressed	Theorized
Sobbed	Struggled	Thirsted
Softened	Studied	Thought
Solicited	Stumbled	Threatened
Solved	Stuttered	Thundered
Soothed	Submitted	Thwarted
Sorted	Substantiated	Timed
Sounded	Succumbed	Tittered
Spared	Suggested	Toasted
Sparred	Sulked	Told
Sparked	Summed	Tolerated
Spat	Summarized	Tormented
Specified	Summoned	Tortured
Speculated	Supplicated	Totaled
Spilled	Supposed	Touted
Spluttered	Surmised	Toyed
Spoke	Surrendered	Trailed
Spooked	Surveyed	Translated
Spouted	Sustained	Transmitted
Spurned	Swaggered	Treasured
Sputtered	Swelled	Trembled